5 Stars for 5 Years!

The contents are definitely worth it and I am very impressed.

Germaine Anderson, The Homeschool Bookmark

I love reading your book. Very informative and it is one of the best among many I purchased about homeschooling.

Zsolt, NH

How is it possible that Lorraine Curry wrote in one book what others have attempted in so many?

Deborah Deggs Cariker, former Houston area star reporter

I thoroughly enjoyed reading your EasyHomeschooling Techniques, even with all the religious references. Had it been available and had I realized I could teach my own children at home I certainly would have used it as a guide.

Rebecca Brown, www.rebeccasreads.com

I've been devouring Easy Homeschooling Companion. Thank you for writing it! I'm also re-reading Easy Homeschooling Techniques today. Both titles are giving (re-giving) me the direction that I'm needing! THANK YOU!!

Deb, NE

My doubts disappeared, replaced with a peace, knowing that I made the right choice. I thank you so much for the "tools."

Jo Ann

I LOVE my book. . . . Thank you for getting me thinking, re-organized and motivated again!!
    Pat, GA

The book was wonderful. . . . Thank you for the encouragement and push into the right direction.
    Debbie Burkett

Easy Homeschooling Techniques *by Lorraine Curry has some unique aspects I have seen in no other homeschooling book.*
    Mary Collis, Home School Favourites, Australia

I have read chapter 1 about 20 times! It is the one book that I am recommending to anyone considering homeschooling. The book is one of those life-changing books—if you read it and follow its guidelines, it will change your life (unless you already do all of this). If I had one word to describe what the book teaches it would be "focus."
    Edie Molder

I absolutely LOVE this book! I already have a copy, but I often lend it out, and then I really miss it!
    Linda, CA

I have read it twice! After seven years of homeschooling I have learned that the most expensive or most time consuming teaching method is not always the best. You book makes that SO clear. It was also very encouraging.
    Millie in CA

I just got the sample copy, and sat down and read two sections . . . the ones on methods and home businesses. If the rest of the book is this good, you've got a winner.
    Mary Hood, *The Relaxed Home Schooler*

Bite-size, manageable chapters bursting with information . . . something for everyone.

Shari Henry, author of *Homeschooling: The Middle Years*

It was your book that made it look so easy to homeschool, that my daughter and I are pulling my three grandchildren out of public school.

Patricia A. Saye, "Lady Liberty"

Wealth of important information.

Kathy Reynolds, *The Home School Gazette*

I LOVE your book!!!!

Penni, MA

It is wonderful! It gives real, simple advice that can help avoid burnout while homeschooling.

Debbie, IL

I've gotten so much encouragement from your book. . . . God bless you.

Renee

An EXCELLENT resource for beginning homeschoolers and veterans alike! Highly recommended.

Robin Nash, The Mustard Seed.

A superb job.

Laurie Hicks, author of *Simply Phonics* & *Simply Spelling*.

Lorraine Curry has a gift for making homeschooling easy! This book is no exception. Chapters are short, manageable for the mom needing help and needing it QUICKLY! Whether you are new to homeschooling, wanting to get off to a good start; or you have homeschooled for more years than you can count, this book will have much to offer. I found myself making excuses to curl up to read just ONE more chapter!

www.lifetimebooksandgifts.com

I can't remember if I let you know how much I LOVE your book! It was such a breath of fresh air! I have been VERY impressed with it. It was such a delight for me. You KNOW it is a great book when a veteran is just as encouraged as a newbie!

Cindy Rushton, author, publisher of *Time for Tea*

I guess my excitement stems from the many books I've read and gotten nowhere with . . . something about the way yours is written . . . your book spoke to me in a way that none of the others have . . . it's so easy to follow—all the symbols you put in there to mark what goes in a notebook were very helpful.

Dee, FL

Lots of great stuff. Many more goodies than just techniques for teaching. Lorraine believes that home education does not have to mimic institutional school . . . also doesn't believe in letting students "do their own thing" without accountability. Methods are quite similar to Charlotte Mason with an emphasis on lots of reading and research. Tells HOW to implement a low stress education without blowing the budget. I learned new things, and it reaffirmed several points on which I was shaky . . . definitely worth a read, and a re-read at that.

Virginia Knowles, *The Hope Chest*

God's Gardener
we plant ★ we water ★ He grows
Boelus NE 68820 USA

EASY Homeschooling Techniques

by Lorraine Curry

Easy Homeschooling Techniques

Scripture quotations, unless otherwise specified, are from the *King James Version* of the Bible.

Definitions, unless otherwise specified, are derived from the *American Heritage Electronic Dictionary* © 1993, Houghton, Mifflin Co.

Book design, layout and illustration—Lorraine Curry
   Ilustrations based on Curry family photos.

"Jessica's Favorites" booklist—Jessica Curry Jobes

"SpillMilk"— Ethan/www.fonthead.com

Remembering

My Mother
Clara Roszczynialski Stobbe

Her generosity in my inheritance provided the finances for the first edition of this book. What a legacy! Her gift continues in mulitple lives.

Recognizing

My Family

Without you there would be no homeschool nor homeschooling books. Only the Lord can reveal the true depth of my love for you!

Thanking

Caren Cornell

Without your encouragement, this first EasyHomeschooling book might never have been. You have been a faithful and true friend.

Special Thanks To

Jean Hall
Melissa Worcester

I have learned from your expertise! Thank you for your willingness and faithfulness to the Easy Homeschooling book projects.

Most of All

I am thanking my God who is the source for everthing I have needed, now need or will need in the future, including life, health, finances, peace, love and joy!

Contents

We Begin • A Practical Guide • A Better Way • A Christian Book • Simplify • Three Basic Methods • EasyHomeschooling

Take an Adventure • List Motives • Dream Dreams • Set Goals • Commit • Form your Philosophy

Prepare • Make Time • Disconnect the Distractions • Tackle the Time Robbers • Build on the Rock • Enjoy Easy Preschool • Free Phonics • The 3Rs • Learn Together • Study the Bible

Save Money • Save Time • Read Aloud • Use the Library • Choose Literature • Prepare • Workbooks and Texts • The Basics • Achieve Excellency

Are you Qualified?

❑ I love my children.
❑ I have, or can make, some time each day to spend with them.
❑ I have strong beliefs not taught in public schools.
❑ I can probably do better than public schools.
❑ I can read and write.
❑ I usually commit to things I believe in.

Did you check most of the boxes? You are qualified to homeschool!

Dingbat Key

✔ Teaching tip or technique
✗ General tip or technique
•➔ Notebook activity
☆ Especially important statement
❀ See more in *Easy Homeschooling Companion*
✍ Vintage or out of print book
☞ If bolded, look in the back of the book.
✐ New in this 3rd edition

What a Little Girl Should Be Taught

- To cook plain wholesome food
- To make her own clothes
- To be neat and orderly
- To care for her own room
- To learn well the art of housekeeping
- To care for her person
- To exercise a quiet reserve in the presence of boys and men
- That all cheap talk is unbecoming
- That loose jokes about "beaux" and "lovers" are improper
- That modesty is a priceless treasure, and will prove her surest protector
- That her brothers are better escorts than most other young men
- That her mother is her best companion and counselor
- That her dress should be plain and not the chief subject of her thoughts or conversation
- That she should wear only such styles of clothing as will cover her person modestly
- That it is better to be useful than ornamental
- That there will be time enough to learn fancy work after she has learned to darn stockings
- That the old rule, "A place for everything and everything in its place," is a good one
- That she should dress for health and comfort as well as for appearance

Home and Health © 1907, Pacific Press Publishing

What a Little Boy Should Be Taught

- To be strong and brave—a little man
- To shun evil companions
- To respect gray hairs
- To be gentle
- To be courteous
- To be prompt
- To be industrious
- To be truthful
- To be honest
- To prefer the companionship of his sisters over other girls
- To honor his father and mother
- To be temperate
- To discard profanity
- To be thoughtful and attentive
- To keep himself pure
- To be his sister's protector
- To refuse to listen to vulgar jokes or stories
- To use common tools skillfully
- To care for his own room
- To do all kinds of housework
- To earn money and to take care of it
- To be neat and orderly in his habits and appearance
- To be self-reliant
- To be his father's partner

Home and Health © 1907, Pacific Press Publishing

Foreword

When Lorraine sent me an earlier edition of this book, I sat down and read the whole thing, which I didn't really have time to do. I had the feeling I was reading all the how-to books boiled down into one volume. This book is concise: Lorraine won't waste your time telling you things you already know. But she will show you how to keep school from being an expensive, confusing operation that leaves you tearing your hair out. She has included detailed courses of study for each grade, excerpts from vintage books, author and poet lists, schedule planners and a list of free or inexpensive resources. Briefly and clearly, she explains how to make sense of various homeschooling methods, lay a good foundation and set goals that you can meet. She'll give you six ways to tell if you are qualified to homeschool, identify time robbers, help you choose good literature for your children and encourage you to read classic novels to even your youngest children. She'll help you see you can learn to draw and paint with your children and why it's important. She even discusses cleaning, making a peaceful home with obedient children, teaching with old books and old-fashioned methods and training your child for eternity! I loved this book! Reading it may give you the confidence you've been needing. A wonderful gift for a new or veteran homeschooler. It would be a special comfort to someone who is being pressured by family or friends and has begun to lose sight of the big picture.

Tammy Duby
www.tobinslab.com

Preface

As you grow, Jessie, you will be trained in the way that God wants you to go . . . I love you, Dad. —August 5, 1983

I forced open my heavy eyelids and looked around the dimly lit room. Would that baby ever stop crying? The pale green walls were about to enfold me in deep sleep. But wait—that was my baby! It had to be! The tiny hospital's nursery had been empty as we passed earlier that evening.

Soon that baby was snuggled quietly in my arms, and I was in the midst of life's most wondrous experience. An experience—amazingly—I never would have chosen. But Jesus is Lord of my life, and that night I learned, once again, that His ways are not our ways—they are much better! Before long, three other precious children were placed by a loving God under our sheltering wings. How then could we tear them out from that protected place and entrust their care and education to anyone else? No one else could love them as we did! Besides—we had a mandate from God. We knew that obedience to God equals blessing. I also knew—from personal experience—how a life without God could result in heartache and sorrow. How then could we place our sweet children in God-less government schools?

But me?—a *teacher*? I never wanted anything to do with education! My fondness for art and design made "education" seem bland and boring.

✐ **However, my children's well being was more important than my inclinations.** Yet, I still refused to consider a structured curriculum. Simple techniques evolved that resulted in children rich in skills and knowledge. In fact, God blessed all of us beyond what we could have imagined or achieved for ourselves. *In every thing ye are enriched by him* (I Cor. 1:5).

A Practical Guide for the Beginner

This book was written as a technique manual for the beginner. It begins at the beginning, details simple techniques and gives step by step instructions. It answers questions, such as:

- "What do I buy?"
- "What can I skip?"
- "How can I simplify the methods, materials and advice?"
- "What do I do first?"
- "How do I do it?"
- "Why should I avoid a structured or full curriculum?"
- "Can I really homeschool through high school?"

You will soon learn how to start and operate a homeschool that will rival the best schools in the nation. This book explains the "nuts and bolts" of this method called *EasyHomeschooling*. You can homeschool, whether you are rich, poor, poorly educated or even employed outside of your home—and the payoff is excellence, with minimal effort. ☆ *Do not spend a dime, or saddle yourself with unnecessary stress, until you read this book!*

A Better Way for the Experienced

Are you already homeschooling? Do you feel overwhelmed because of what you think you must do to educate your children? Are you marooned on Methods Island, trying to make sense of them all? Are you drowning under a deluge of educational materials? The catalogs keep getting bigger and bigger while the decisions become more and more difficult. Even reading the giant curriculum guides takes valuable time.

Are you using a structured curriculum? Do you really enjoy your lessons—and their preparation? Are the courses pushing too much? Are your children really learning anything?

Perhaps you have been using the unit study approach. How much time do you spend in preparation? And in "school"? Is this much time really necessary for quality education?

Are you searching for a method that will draw your family closer? Independent studies and computer courses can pull family members in different directions.

Which method will draw your family closer?

A Christian Book

Jesus Christ changed my life dramatically many years ago. Jesus Christ daily loads us with benefits (Ps. 68:19) and is faithful to answer every prayer as we stand in faith. Because of His death for my sins, and resurrection from the dead, I have a guarantee that the blessings will not end with this life. I would consider no other lifestyle nor philosophy.

Even if my beliefs differ from yours, we *do* agree about wanting the best for our children. This is a practical book—a how-to book. If my faith is revealed through its pages, I make no apologies. My goal for this particular book is not to share my faith but to share the method of educating called *EasyHomeschooling*. Nevertheless, I write as a Christian to other Christians—because as homeschoolers, Christians are the majority.

Materials

Have you ever gone to a store needing one item, and found yourself detained hesitating among an overwhelming array of manufacturer's brands? The vast assortment of homeschooling materials now available can make things extremely confusing. Homeschooling does not have to be so complicated! EasyHomeschooling is a simple—yet high quality—method of educating. Moreover, this method offers tips and suggestions for low-cost alternatives. Homeschooling can even be free! This book tells how. But because most of us want to purchase some books and materials, I give certain materials a stamp of approval and even produce and sell some items through our business ☞ **God's Gardener.** But the choice—whether to spend, or not to spend—is yours!

Do you want to be frugal or free with cash?

Three Basic Methods

The maze of methods can be simplified by sorting them into three basic groups: unschooling, structured schooling and a style of schooling that I will call watershed schooling.

Unschooling

John Holt—whose books are available at libraries—was the father of unschooling, the first method of the modern homeschooling movement. Bill Greer of ☞ **F.U.N. News** says that unschoolers want ". . . to keep alive the spark of curiosity and the natural love of learning with which all children are born."[1]

The idea behind unschooling is that individuals learn best when they are free to seek knowledge about personal interests. I found this true in my own life. My knowledge store accumulated only when I had a personal interest in—and sought out information about—a particular subject. The sum of what I learned during structured schooling could have been taught in a year or two. (If there had been more reading aloud from interesting books throughout my youth, things might have been different!)

Unschooling is a hands-off method. In pure unschooling the parent acts as teacher only when the child expresses interest in a particular topic—then merely aids the child in finding the resources he or she needs. Mark and Helen Hegener, publisher and editor of ☞ *Home Education Magazine,* say:

> *Our children have always been completely responsible for their own learning, from the ABC's on up. They've known from day one that they've had our complete and loving support, and that we'd be here to help them whenever they asked for it. There's been no delineation in our family between "learning" and "living." As we live, we learn. It's as simple as that.*[2]

Dr. Raymond and Dorothy Moore in their book, ☞ *The Successful Homeschool Family Handbook*, report on a well-funded study done many years ago which gives a gold star to unschooling. "The children who were not formally taught at all had the highest scores in all areas measured."[3]

Structured Schooling

Most of us know structured schooling well because we are its products! Structured homeschoolers have just moved the school into their homes—sometimes even moved a teacher into their homes with videos. The structured homeschoolers purchase their books, materials and teacher's guides from one company or from similar curriculum companies. Such books usually have an abundance of data in them that the students are expected to read and retain, but alas! students promptly forget most everything they have read. I know—I was schooled this way and also witnessed our daughters' lack of retention when they used these books. Although the books are sometimes beautiful and interesting, permanent learning is rare with a structured curriculum.

Watershed Schooling

A watershed is a ridge of high land dividing two areas that are drained by different river systems. A watershed is also a critical point that marks a division. I'm christening this group watershed because it is midway between unschooling and structured schooling. Watershed parents usually, in their own words, pick and choose curricula. Some make their own plans and schedules and teach whatever they want. Others loosely follow the plan of a chosen method. They sometimes focus on the child's interest—as in unschooling—but more often the teacher decides what she wants her children to learn. She may have a schedule, or may just do school when it is convenient. These parents are usually flexible in what, where, why and how, and yet not so flexible that they give the child complete control—as in pure unschooling. Often much time is spent in reading aloud. There are more homeschoolers in this third group than in any other.[4] Some examples are *Charlotte Mason*, *Far Above Rubies*, *Five In A Row*, *KONOS*, and *EasyHomeschooling*.

EasyHomeschooling

Although other methods have given good results, all methods are not equal. EasyHomeschooling techniques such as planning, combining, using the library and reading aloud unite to produce high quality education without large expenditures of time or money.

Just as EasyHomeschooling provides maximum education in minimum time, the mission of this book is to provide maximum information in a minimum of words. I have chosen to leave out socialization and laws, as well as lengthy personal experiences, so that I can focus on what *you* will do in your own successful homeschool. By following the suggestions in this book, you will save its price, many, many times over. May *Easy Homeschooling Techniques* inspire your thoughts and actions and be always completely usable.

Lorraine Curry
www.easyhomeschooling.com

Since you will be learning with your children, I have used the pronoun, "you" interchangeably to represent you or your children. Many times you will want to have your child do the suggested activity. Other times you will do it together.

1
Laying Foundations

Thank you Lord, for this new adventure in your service. Thank you that you have called me to this. —February 20, 1989

I lay on the beach, gasping for breath. I was a body surfer and even Maui's huge winter storm waves couldn't keep me home! The exhilaration was worth the battering. In college, I wanted to skydive, but my father wouldn't grant permission—a friend's son had been killed when his parachute failed to open. Later, I was enticed by the opportunity to succeed in life insurance sales and became the first female member of our company's President's Cabinet. I've welcomed most challenges, but succeeding at this task of raising children has been life's biggest challenge—and its greatest adventure.

By definition, an adventure is an undertaking that includes uncertainty. Are you asking yourself, "Is homeschooling the best choice for my child? . . . Can I *really* do this?" I never really considered whether I was qualified to teach my own children. My desire to keep them home was so strong, I knew that I would find a way.

An adventure is often—by its uncertain nature—an exciting experience. There are surprises ahead that you don't even know about yet!

Homeschooling can be a financial speculation or risk—somewhat like a business venture. The word "speculation" makes it sound as if homeschooling is risky. But homeschoolers everywhere prove that this "venture" is a sure thing!

I wanted to protect them from the wild world!

List Motives

There are several good reasons to homeschool. I wanted my children to have a better education than I had. I felt like we could do better than the schools. I wanted them to know the truth of God's Word that would set them free—as it had me. I wanted to spare them the awful consequences of a life lived without God. I wanted to protect them from the wild world. I just wanted them to be home, not off somewhere else. My husband and I wanted to obey God. Why do you want to homeschool?

Notebook Planning

•• Get a notebook or diary. You can use a three-ring binder, loose-leaf notebook paper and at least five tabbed dividers or a thick divided spiral notebook. ✐ I now have a *Busy Woman's Daily Planner* with pages that seem to be made for this system. For help in choosing the planner and pages that will work best for you call **800-848-7715** or visit ***www.thebusywoman.com***

Write your motives (reasons) for wanting to homeschool on the first page of your notebook. I think you will enjoy this list-making process as you *write the vision, and make it plain* (Hab. 2:2). These planning techniques will build a foundation that will make homeschooling easier and more focused.[1]

Now go to the second page and make a list of your values. A value is *a principle, standard, or quality considered worthwhile or desirable*. Some values are a strong family, a close relationship with God, a consistently loving attitude and untarnished integrity.

Dream Dreams

➥ Label your first index tab "Dreams." List your dreams for yourself and your family. This activity should be done over a period of time, such as several days, as you pray and add to the list. Make sure you have everything, even those dreams that seem totally out of reach. Our God says, *Behold, I am the LORD, the God of all flesh: is there any thing too hard for me* (Jer. 32:27)?

My notebook lists the following:

- I would see my children grown into fine young adults.
- I would be a designer in my own manufacturing company.
- I would write and publish several books, including an autobiography, how-to's and novels.
- I would have wealth to give generously to God's work.
- I would glorify God by using my creativity.

This list gives ideas and examples of the types of dreams that you can put on your list. Look over your own dreams list and check to see if your dreams are in line with your values. Either cross off those that aren't or star those that are. But don't be too hasty—another name for dreams is desires.

Delight thyself also in the LORD; and he shall give thee the desires of thine heart (Ps. 37:4). *It is your Father's good pleasure to give you the kingdom* (Luke 12:32). *If ye be willing and obedient, ye shall eat the good of the land* (Is. 1:19).

Think about all the people you could help if you had more money. Very large budgets are needed to preach the "good news" today. Your family might be the one the Lord wants to use to help meet the world's needs!

Set Goals

Goals are definite results that can be achieved within a certain period of time. Long term goals might be achieved within five years; short term within one. No need to list your long term and short term goals separately. These lists work. After three months, I had achieved

almost half of my top goals; after six, I crossed off more!
- ~~Start up business.~~
- ~~Run business.~~
- ~~Become organized.~~
- ~~Sell land.~~
- ~~Pay off credit cards.~~
- ~~Touch every home in our town for Christ.~~
- Pray habitually, using prayer list.
- Teach children to be self starters, accountable to God.
- Finish restoring house.

This is not my complete goal list. I have combined major goals for illustration purposes. Several completed goals will lead to fulfillment of your dreams. Again, take time to get your thoughts crystallized. Don't rush this process. When you get your goals down on paper and see a pattern emerging, it will be clearer why you have considered home-schooling.

➻ Label your second index divider "Goals." Following the examples, list your own goals. You may make separate lists of personal goals, homeschooling goals and business goals, along with goals for each of your children. Choose your top ten goals from your lists and star each or list these top goals on a separate piece of paper. These will be the goals that you will work on first. Place this list in the front of your goal section. If you have made lists for your children, choose one or two important goals for each of them.

At least once a year, review and revise both your dream list and your goal list. At that time you may decide that a particular dream or goal wasn't as important as you once thought. Eliminate it from your list and replace it with any new dreams and goals you want to add.

Commitment

Next, it is time to prayerfully consider commitment. If we go into major personal relationships without commitment, the relationship usually fails. Homeschooling also requires serious commitment. First, take the time to find out just what it is that God wants for you and your family. Remember, you *can do all things through Christ.* (Phil. 4:13).

There is a method for reaching your goals. There are steps to take that will lead to the fulfillment of your dreams. In Chapter 5, "Planning for Success," you will learn how to schedule those steps. When you work your step lists, your goals will be met and surpassed, almost automatically. In the meantime, pray about committing to this life choice for your family. This book will make your commitment effortless, as you discover that homeschooling can be simple and natural.

➥ Enter your commitment statement or pledge on the very first page of your notebook along with your motive statement.

✐ This is *such* an important step! If you will not commit—especially to Biblical parenting and scheduling principles (described more fully in ❀ *Easy Homeschooling Companion*) I cannot wholeheartedly recommend homeschooling. Your child might be better off elsewhere.

Educational Philosophy

Why educate? If you have read about home education, you may have already formulated some opinions, but don't be too quick to define your educational philosophy. An example is Charlotte Mason's. She said, "It is the business of education to find some way of supplementing the weakness of will which is the bane of most of us, as of the children."[2]

Here's another:

An education isn't how much you have committed to memory, or even how much you know. It's being able to differentiate between what you do know and what you don't. It's knowing where to go to find out what you need to know; and it's knowing how to use the information once you get it. . . .[3]

Why should we educate anyhow?

✐ For more ideas on the philosophy of education, see Chapter 10, "Gleaning from History."

•◦ After you have formulated your educational philosophy, write it in the front pages of your notebook. When you have laid the foundation by listing your motives, commitment pledge, educational philosophy and values in the first pages of your notebook and your dreams and goals in their own sections, you are ready to go on and start your very own successful homeschool!

2
Starting Up

Started "school" this month. —February 20, 1989

ephi, at five, amazed her aunt and uncle with her perfect reading. "Perhaps," my *public-school-educator* sister offered, "she should have the advantages of the special resources of schools." Although I highly respected her opinions and had been greatly influenced by her previously, this time God's call to homeschooling was stronger than her advice. The fact is, the mother is the perfect teacher for her own children because she loves them more than anyone else ever could. The father, of course, is also qualified and responsible for teaching his own children.

Can you read? You can teach your children to read. Can you write? You can teach them to write. You can teach your children to teach themselves, even though you may not know a subject well. You can read and learn, and share what you've learned. You can learn along with them! Qualifications are minimal to guide your children into educational excellence.

Legal Requirements

Homeschooling is legal in every state. Information can be obtained from your state's Department of Education or from the ☞ **Home School Legal Defense Association.** Some homeschooling books include this information—but be sure it is current. I found extremely outdated legal requirements in our library's copy of ☞ *The Home School Manual* by Theodore Wade. (It was the library's oversight, not Mr. Wade's—he regularly publishes new editions!)

Some states might allow you to choose what day of the year, days of the week and hours of the day you want to homeschool. Along with a minimum number of hours required, you might also need to sign and notarize forms stating your firmly held religious beliefs. Some states require a a scope and sequence if one does not use a recognized curriculum. A scope and sequence details what one plans to teach each year and in what order the topics will be presented. See Chapter 5, "Planning for Success," for more about the scope and sequence, including instructions for creating it.

If the parent uses a structured curriculum package from a major publisher, a scope and sequence may not be required. Although this may be easier when submitting information, the day-to-day use of a full curriculum is definitely more difficult and time-consuming. It is also the same ineffective style of educating that has been used in schools for years. This method attempts to pour facts and figures into the student, hoping that some will "stick." It allows no room for individuality, but rather molds each student into a "clone" of the next one. Since I am a creative type, I hated this type of education as a youth and wasn't about to tackle it, nor shackle my children with it. With *EasyHomeschooling,* you can forget the bother and expense of using a traditional curriculum with its hefty and formidable teacher's guides!

Prepare!

Before you actually start schooling, some preparations need to be made. Along with making time and preparing spiritually, there is "preschool"—but this preschool is not what you would expect! There is also the preparation of organizing the home which you will learn in Chapter 4. Because this startup is so easy and gradual, you can delay your organization until later, but if you feel you just must have order now, jump to "Making Order" first, and then come back here.

Make Time

If homeschooling is started with young children, there is a gradual building of routines—and very little time required—because subjects can be introduced one at a time.[1]

If you are taking your child out of an institutional school, there might be more time required, but not as much as you might think. To make more time, set your priorities and eliminate distractions.

Disconnect the Distractions

✐ Some of my closest friends and family members say I am far too radical about TV and movies (and the KJV Bible). I would not be radical if these things were not a matter of life and death to Christians, our nation and the world, and I believe they are. I do not judge those who watch TV, I just don't understand. Even though I watch occasionally I come away more repulsed and determined that it is not for the Christian. Think about it! Where did the majority of criminals first see criminal activity? Where did the majority of youth first see fornication as acceptable and even "proper"? Why is the occult and the "supernatural" more acceptable today than even twenty or thirty years ago? Why are the churches so dried up and dead? Why have all these things overtaken us? Christians are not praying, but why? There is a Christian gift called discernment, but the Lord warns that we will become dull of hearing. ★ *TV has made us deaf and blind.*

Learn not the way of the heathen.—Jer. 10:2

At the very least, TV and videos are time robbers. Although there are a few worthwhile programs and videos, the value of these—in my opinion—can never outweigh their detriment. Thirty years of research show that ninety percent of achievement in school is determined by how much TV a child watches.[2] The separate hemispheres of the brain have different functions. If one is stimulated more in the developmental

TV trains your children in worldy ways.

stage (from ages two to twelve), the other could be stunted. The nature of TV dumbs down children, causing low attention span and creating the need for simplistic (instead of rich and classic) subject matter. Other negative effects on children are less sensitivity to the pain and suffering of others, greater fear of the world around them and increased likelihood of engaging in aggressive or harmful behavior. Many of you know exactly what I am talking about, because you have seen these effects in your own children. Consider these facts and predictions from *The Futurist* magazine:

> *Television is absorbing increasing amounts of people's free time . . . . [It is] entertainment without any need to associate with other people. . . . [It] deprives people of the social learning acquired during group entertainment. In the days before television and computers, face-to-face conversation was the primary means of entertainment, pursued around the dinner table at home. . . . This social entertainment trained people to deal with other people, to respect their interests . . . . The rise of electronic entertainment seems to have been accompanied by increasing rudeness . . . will tend to desocialize people, making them more prone to antisocial and criminal behavior . . . a non-society—a poorly integrated mass of electronic hermits, unable to work well together because we no longer play together. Institutions . . . will face the challenge of seeking support from people whose loyalty is almost entirely to themselves.[3]*

Even if there is nothing offensive about what one is watching, vulgar advertising can be flashed so quickly before pure and precious eyes that it is impossible to prevent access to this window of the soul.

✐ Who is the enemy here? Let's not forget to pray for all involved in media and entertainment and against the one who delights in stealing our children.

Along with TV, computers and online activities can also interfere with family solidarity and waste time. Soon after World War II, science fiction writings predicted "that people might become the slaves of machines . . . might begin to think differently, submit to computers, lose judgment, become spiritually shallow, unhappy and unable to cope with jobs and daily lives dominated by technology."[4]

Having a computer requires self-control and wisdom. Contrary to popular opinion, it is not essential for a quality education. Your child will learn computer skills quickly when needed. There are so many better things to do—books to read, walks and picnics to go on, chores to do together, independent discovery—the list is endless.

Other Time Robbers

Do you (or your children) spend a lot of time reading catalogs or magazines? Are your days spent on the telephone or shopping? Life is too short to waste. (Ps. 90:12)

Plan to spend the greatest portion of your time on the activites that will help you reach your goals. In Chapter 5, you will learn to list these activities as steps to your goals (step lists).

➡ Take a one or two week inventory of exactly how you spend every hour of every day. You may see a whole lot of time that could be better spent.

The Solid Rock

"A hurried glance at Christ snatched after lying abed too late will never effect a radical transformation of character."[5]

Christians know that the foundation of life is God's Word. The Word should be the foundation of the Christian homeschool too. The most important activity in all endeavors—and in your homeschooling effort—is a habitual quiet time. I thought I didn't have time when my children were small, but I found it an absolute necessity to make time, somehow. I had to trust God to give me the rest that I needed, even if I got up very early.

Secure your foundation before you actually begin teaching your children. If you have many small children and many demands on your life, hang on—it does get easier! Our four children were very close in age, so I know what some of you are going through. But our girls started helping at a young age, and eventually did so much of the housework, that I was able to do projects such as book writing! Wait on the Lord—there is a time and season for everything. Which brings me to counsel you not to rush into homeschooling when your children are too young.

How do you know when they are too young? Resistance to instruction is a good sign. Be sensitive to your child and ask the Lord, expecting His answer.

✐ Most of all, *enjoy* those precious little ones—how I long to be able to return to those days you are now experiencing. They are truly the best days of your life!

Easy Preschool

You have prepared by praying, thinking, listening, listing, making time and possibly making order. Now we will begin schooling. You don't have to leave home. You don't have to buy toys, games or snacks. You don't have to expose your children to other children's germs. At this preschool you cuddle in with your little ones and read lots of good books. That's it! This is the *EasyHomeschooling* preschool. Simple, isn't it?

You do not have to spend hundreds of dollars when you begin to homeschool. Do not overwhelm yourself and your child with an excess of material. Easy does it. The best materials are often those that you already have in your home.

Bible

The earliest American schools had two textbooks. These schools used the Bible for history, literature, spelling, science, grammar and reading; and a hymnal for music reading, singing and writing music. Read at least one chapter a day from the Bible to even your youngest child. Your children will begin to learn morals, character and many other important things (see Chapter 8, "Training for Eternity"). Using the *King James Version* of the Bible will also give them a very strong start in English skills. See more early-learning tips for teaching the Bible in ❀ *Easy Homeschooling Companion,* especially in Chapter 5, "Harvesting from History."

Ban TV! Break out the Books!

Professionals and intellectuals agree that the most important thing a parent can do for their child's education is to read to them. The one common factor found in all children who learned to read without being formally taught was not high IQ, not high family income, not parents who had college degrees, but rather "all these children were read to by their parents regularly, frequently, and from whatever materials happened to be at hand—newspapers, road signs, even packing labels."[6]

If you do an abundance of reading aloud, your children will learn spelling, grammar, vocabulary and style without being formally taught.

It may be—especially if your child has watched much TV or many videos—that he or she will find it difficult to concentrate when you read aloud. If this is the case, ban video and start reading simple books on an interesting subject. The longer the fast from visual stimulation, the more their hunger for words develops. They will desire the mental stimulation of words and the enjoyable process of making their own mind pictures. May I suggest Beatrix Potter's well written and illustrated titles such as *Peter Rabbit*. Other options are vintage books about animals by Thornton Burgess (reprints available from ☞ **Dover**) or

Arthur Scott Bailey (***www.hstreasures.com***). These will hold a young child's interest, expand intelligence and whet his appetite for good books.

An easy startup technique is to introduce the basics one at a time. Make sure your child knows phonics well before going on to reading. When he can read fluently, begin handwriting exercises. Creative writing can only be done after handwriting is learned. (Pre-writing *can* be done, and is explained below.) Finally, begin simple math. An exception is combining spelling with phonics. See more in Chapter 6, "Combining Subjects."

Early childhood is the best time to begin establishing and maintaining habits—especially health habits such as brushing and flossing teeth, bathing regularly and washing face and hands as needed.

Phonics

Achievement in all subjects will be built upon thoughtful reading. Skill in reading starts with a mastery of phonics. Public education's failure is most obvious in this area as parents often purchase phonics materials and reteach their children the most basic of skills—when the school has had all day to do it. Look at what else parents are supposed to do.

[They should] . . . talk to their children about school and homework, read with them, go to the library, have books at home and ensure that their children attend school daily. "I'd like parents to go into the school and be involved with the teacher, the principal, the PTA . . . ."[7]

Whew! Talk about overtaxing already stressed parents! You will do it right the first time by teaching your child yourself. (Homeschooling is also a more economical solution—public schools spend an average of $5,325 per student per year![8])

✐ Although the "No Child Left Behind" program has attempted to solve the problems, according to recent reports they are experiencing "growing pains."

The Reading Solution

The solution to the reading problem is phonics. We used the same copy of ☞ *Alpha-phonics* by Samuel Blumenfeld for each of our children. Actually I used it for only three of our four, because Zephi sat in on her older sister's lessons and learned to read on her own. Several years ago, the book cost us around twenty dollars. It was one of our best buys considering the great value of reading and the per-student cost. The book was very easy to use. ☞ *Simply Phonics* is similar to *Alpha-Phonics*. It can be used for one to three years and will take your child step by step through letter sounds and word families. When your child finishes the book, he or she is able to read!

Soon your child will be able to read!

✔ A free *EasySchool* technique is to do it yourself without a book. Start with the lower case (small letters) because text is primarily lower case. Later your child will learn to read the upper case.

Using a pencil and paper (or a dry-erase marker board or chalk board), teach the sound of each letter, starting with the short vowels. (✐ Always speak as clearly as possible.) Add some consonants—one at a time—to make simple words such as *cat* and *dog*. Next teach the vowel combinations such as *ae* and *oi*. Other consonant combinations such as *ch* and *st* should be taught along with all the rest of the consonants. Finally, teach long vowels, long vowel combinations and words with silent *e* at the end such as "gate."

To help your child blend the sounds of letters into words, use a simple playground slide diagram. At the top of the slide write the beginning letter or combination, and at the bottom, the rest of the word. "Make the 'ch' go down the slide and run into the 'at'!" Keep it simple by teaching only the sounds of the letters. Later your child can learn the names—perhaps when long vowels are learned. Teach the usual sounds of the letters—do not confuse your child by teaching rules or exceptions now. If they ask, just tell them they will learn those later,

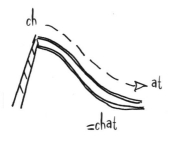

identifying them as "rule breakers." If your little geniuses are really interested in these exceptions, have them list them in a notebook!

Here is a simplified sequence for teaching phonics. Teach the sounds consecutively. Make sure your child gets plenty of practice reading words that fit each pattern.

1) short *a, e, i, o, u;* and *y* sounding as a short vowel
2) consonant sounds (all the rest of the letters)
3) consonant clusters such as *ch, th, st*
4) broad *o: au, aw, al*
5) other clusters: *oi, oy, ou, ow; oo; ar, er, ir, or, ur*
6) long vowel clusters: *ea, ee, ai, oa, ow*
7) long vowels: words that end in silent e
8) *c* followed by *e, i* or *y* says "s"
9) *g* followed by *e, i* or *y* may say "j"

✓ For drill, make your own flash cards. Use three by five inch blank index cards, scrap cardboard or white poster board cut to size. Write one large letter or combination (*sh, pl, ch,* etc.) on each card. Have your child say the sound. Later put these cards together to form simple words.

Practice Makes Perfect

As soon as your child knows how to read, he or she needs practice. Get simple phonics-based readers such as *Hop on Pop* from the library or *Bob Books* from ☞ **Scholastic.** But don't try to use *Dick and Jane*! These books have so many sight words in them, they will only frustrate your new reader. By using *McGuffey's Readers*—received free as an introductory offer from a book club—our girls were two grade levels ahead of other homeschoolers when they were in second grade. They were then reading independently and fluently, so we discontinued *McGuffeys* but kept them for their content. The secret to success with whatever practice materials you choose is regularity. Do something every day, even if it's just for a short time. (Exact replicas of the original 1879 *McGuffey's* are available from ☞ **hstreasures.com**)

Some educational "authorities" would burden us with unnecessary work such as spelling, comprehension, grammar and vocabulary. These do not need to be learned separately! If a child is read to, learns to read phonetically, *is read to,* starts reading fluently, *is read to,* and continues to read individually, that child will learn, and learn well, all the peripherals of our language.

Penmanship

Don't be confused by the styles available. Just choose one and stick with it. We started with traditional and then went to italic. Since our eldest had started with regular cursive she did not do well with italic so we went back to regular cursive for her. All of our other children used italic workbooks. Zephi did calligraphy at eleven. At age fifteen, Jessica finally acquired an attractive hand after more practice with calligraphy and Spencerian. One complaint I hear from my children who have learned italic is that they can't read cursive, although they do eventually figure it out.

✐ Jessica has the best writing as an adult because she had the most practice as a child. Handwriting is important training in neatness and influences achievement in every subject.

✔ Although there are penmanship tablets available, any type of notebook or notebook paper will do. Use two lines or as many as necessary, adapting the size to that which your child is comfortable with. (Have him make a letter first so you can see.) In your best penmanship, write the alphabet in a column to the left of the page and let your child fill out the rest of each line.

✐ Worksheets for penmanship (and for nearly every other subject) can be printed from internet sites. Search for "free worksheets" along with your topic word at *www.google.com.*

Pre-Writing, Writing

✓ Encourage your youngest children to be storytellers. If your child is not able to write yet, take dictation as he or she tells you the story. Your child can then illustrate this story. This is the creative pre-writing I mentioned earlier. When you read to your children from a young age, they will be natural writers.

Copywork is an effective technique for the young child. Either write the passage for your child to copy or let him copy directly from a book. By doing copywork, your child will learn style and grammar from master writers.

When your children are able to write, have them transcribe their own stories. Don't pay any attention to errors at this point. You don't want to discourage them. If they want you to spell the words for them, do it. Eventually they will know more words. At that time, you can point out misspelled words or make a daily or weekly spelling list of those. (See more on spelling in Chapter 6, "Combining Subjects.") Save your students' papers—at least the best ones—you will treasure them someday! If you need help with grammar, get a language handbook from *Scott, Foresman and Company* (800-554-4411) or search *www.amazon.com* or *www.google.com*. You could even use an old or vintage title.

Arithmetic

For precept must be upon precept, precept upon precept; line upon line, line upon line; here a little, and there a little . . . (Is. 28:10).

Children will learn number concepts by taking part in ordinary daily activities. For instance, they can be a big help by counting silverware and setting the table. Some people use beans or other items to teach primary number concepts. Although we used many games and other math materials over the years, we found the simplest tools to be best.

✓ The simplest tools are pencils and paper. Flash cards can be made starting with the easiest equation: 1+1=2. Use daily until the facts are mastered and then occasionally for review. *Calculadder* is a set of master sheets for timed math drills, and also is effective for mastering the math facts. Another great tool is an antique math text. Save time, money and effort by using speed drills and old texts exclusively for the best results with young students. We had great results with *Strayer-Upton Practical Arithmetics,* which are now available as reprints.

Learn With Your Children

After a degree of mastery has been achieved in the basics, you can continue with every other subject and topic by studying together. Subjects that you might have disliked all of your life suddenly come alive. This was my experience with history. When the children and I started reading biographies and other historical books, I discovered history to be quite interesting!

Your Children Learn With You

As a homeschooler, you will do the inconvenient thing, and let your child be your partner in every task you and your husband do. This is the most effective training and learning opportunity. If you do it now, you will be blessed tremendously in the future with hard-working children, more free time and a closer family.

3
EasySchool Basics

I am going through some old school papers and throwing a lot out. If what I have is representative of my education, what a poor education! . . . making way for a new generation of learning . . . God's way and the most excellent way. —January 3, 1989.

I dropped the magazine into my lap and gazed into the distance where Jessica, Ezra and Eli were jumping from the bridge piling into the glistening river. I was dazed—and it wasn't the summer sun. Under *structured* on the cover of this "methods" issue was the word, *easiest*. How could it be? How could they say this method was easier than even the highly successful unschooling? A long-time acquaintance—and brand new homeschooler—had just told me the real facts about the structured method. After wavering for years, she finally plunged in with this "easy" method and was using fifty books for two children and schooling for eight to nine hours each day! Others have told me similar stories. I was mentally weeping for all the beginners who had been lead astray by these two words, when Zephi drew me back with a comment about her engineering feat. She had built a dam in the sand.

What is EasyHomeschooling?

Although you will find *EasyHomeschooling* systems throughout this book, here I will highlight its features, especially those not explained elsewhere. In a nutshell—reading aloud produces great results, while using the library saves money. Free and low cost resources are available; particular techniques and materials encourage excellence.

EasyHomeschoolers learn all the time like unschoolers. We emphasize great books as do those using the Classical method. Reading aloud is a cornerstone, as it is for Charlotte Mason people. We encourage self-study as does Dr. Robinson, and combine subjects as do unit-study enthusiasts. Our students have been accelerated, but without push and shove, without the strain of excess structure. EasyHomeschooling combines the best of the methods with the lowest cost materials.

Save Money

EasyHomeschooling can save you lots of money. Homeschoolers spend an average of over five-hundred dollars each year per child, while public school's average is over five-*thousand* dollars![1]

A recent year's bottom line for us was only fourteen ($14.00) dollars! True, we have ready access to antique books because we sell them, but we also purchased the expensive Robinson CDs that year. How did we do it? In previous years we bought assorted new items and didn't need them anymore so we sold them. But you can save money, even if you have never homeschooled before.

Your tools will include a rich assortment of library books and materials, old and antique books, like-new used materials, leaflets, booklets and art videos. EasyHomeschooling encompasses free or inexpensive do-it-yourself techniques such as how to keep high school credits, set up homemaking classes, train your children to draw and teach math in a unique way.

Save Time

Most of the other methods take much time, as my friend learned in her first year with structured learning. EasyHomeschooling is so time efficient that even a working parent can homeschool! In issue #18 of *Practical Homeschooling* I recommend two or three hours a night and four to five on the weekend. EasyHomeschooling eliminates the "unnecessaries" and focuses on the learning activities that have been proven to give excellent results.

Reading Aloud

"The single most important activity for building the knowledge required for eventual success in reading is reading aloud to children."[2]

Children's success in school is definitely linked to reading skill, which itself springs from early parental involvement. Reading aloud is like leaven that prepares dough for baking. It increases the quality and quantity of brain cells so that a child eventually excels in all educational endeavors, not only in reading. ★ *Reading aloud is the essential activity for all ages.* Do this one thing and you can forget teaching language arts. Your children will begin to read much on their own, acquire a lovely command of the English language and write beautifully. They will use advanced vocabulary, although sometimes mispronounced (a good reason to have your children read aloud, even when older).

✐ *Using the Dictionary.* Although most unknown words will be understood through context (the meaning of the words and sentences around them) it is a good idea to look up unknown words at times when a work—such as a poem or memory scripture—will be reread over several days. Spend a few minutes learning how to understand the symbols that are the key to proper pronunciation and also look up those words that no one knows how to pronounce properly.

Do you want the best, or the rest?

The Best Read-Aloud

The most important book to read aloud is the Bible. Don't settle for second best and read one of the newer versions to your children. When read much and often, the King James Bible will be understood and will give your children a wonderful literary foundation. The KJV Bible was selected by scholars as one of the finest examples of writing style in existence. Other versions give your children a model of poor writing, with grammar and style mistakes.[3]

Most words are understood in context—if they are heard often enough, they will be understood by the way they are used in the sentences. See more about the value and simplicity of the King James Bible in "Training for Eternity," Chapter 8.

Other Books, Other Benefits

✓ Once you are habitually reading the Bible then you can go on to other classic works. These authors will garnish your lives with their lovely prose: Beatrix Potter (*Peter Rabbit* and others), Laura Ingalls Wilder (*Little House on the Prairie* and others), Louisa May Alcott (*Little Women, Little Men, Jo's Boys* and others), Charles Dickens (*David Copperfield, The Christmas Carol,* others), and Mark Twain. We laughed all the way through *Tom Sawyer Abroad,* although sometimes Twain's young characters model character one would rather not see in young 'uns! My girls read a lot of James Herriot's books because they love cats. Try authors and poets like Henry Wadsworth Longfellow, Robert Louis Stevenson, John Greenleaf Whittier and Rudyard Kipling. You don't have to read something just because someone recommends it. If you don't like a work or think it inappropriate for your family, find something better.

Another reason to read aloud—and perhaps even more important than the educational benefit—is to foster family togetherness. You will find that sharing laughter and tears draws your family together. (In our family, Mom is usually the only one with tears!)

How to Choose Literature

Don't waste your time on dumbed-down books. Not every book worth reading will have exquisite language, yet after reading a few paragraphs, you will know whether a particular book will foster excellence or mediocrity.

To choose good literature you can rely on catalog descriptions with comments such as "well-written," "interestingly written," "of literary quality" and so forth. If you can see a book, it is even easier to choose literature. Study the following excerpts so that you will be able to choose fine writing.

- "Mistress Botsford grabbed a heavy skillet and planted herself firmly in the doorway. If they planned to enter unasked, they'd reckon first with her and her frying pan. The riders drew up. Two of them dismounted. Ten remained on their horses." A *We Were There* book from the 50s
- "Those who returned safely went back to the camp at the valley's entrance. But General Jeffries was not there." A *Signature* book. © 1957

The following are from the 1800s or earlier.

- "During the weeks that elapsed while the three great armies were assembling and taking up their positions, the troops stationed round Brussels had a pleasant time of it." *One of the 28th,* G.A. Henty
- "Graham then gave a brief narration of the direful circumstance. He and his father, Lord Dundaff, having crossed the south coast of Scotland in their way homeward, stopped to rest at Ayr." *Scottish Chiefs,* Jane Porter
- "And having administered this rebuke, as though it were something of a chief importance, he turned to examine our defenses. *Kidnapped,* by R. L. Stevenson
- "The time which passes over our heads so imperceptibly, makes the same gradual change in habits, manners, and character, as in personal appearance. At the revolution of every five years we find ourselves another, and yet the same—there is a change of views, and no less of the light in which we regard them; a change of motives as well as of actions." *The Abbot,* Scott
- "Give every man thine ear, but few thy voice: take each man's censure, but reserve thy judgment." *Hamlet,* Shakespeare
- "Now I beheld in my dream, that they had not journeyed far, but the river and the way for a time parted; at which they were not a

little sorry, yet they durst not go out of the way." *Pilgrims Progress*, Bunyan

- "She weepeth sore in the night, and her tears are on her cheeks: among all her lovers she hath none to comfort her; all her friends have dealt treacherously with her, they are become her enemies." *King James Bible*, Jeremiah 1:2

The Public Library

Your library has many beautiful and useful books. If a book is questionable, skip over the objectionable parts. Our children learned that God's Word is the only complete truth and measuring instrument for everything else they read or hear, and just laughed at writings indicating evolution was fact. But when a child is young, the truth needs to be continually re-emphasized. *For precept must be upon precept, precept upon precept; line upon line, line upon line; here a little, and there a little* (Is. 28:10).

I was thrilled to find one fragile copy of *Uncle Tom's Cabin* on a bottom shelf in the back of the library. I even asked to purchase it to protect it from the discard pile! We shared this Christian colossus during our Civil War study. I cried more than once while we were reading it. Andy seems to read the most memorable books—or are they are memorable because "Dad" reads them? More recently we read another book of this caliber during our study of World War II. It was *The Hiding Place* by Corrie ten Boom.

The library saved us a lot of money—thousands of dollars over the years. I can't imagine where we would put all those books if we had bought them, although we have a large bookcase and several smaller ones throughout our house. Of course you may want to purchase some books for gifts, for reference or for building your own library, but unless you like to be lavish with your financial resources, wait—and in a future chapter, I'll give tips on finding the best books. (Chapter 7, "Enjoying Heirlooms") For school, we select books from the library based on our scope and sequence (Chapter 5, "Planning for Success") Some years we use mostly non-fiction for science and history. Other years we use more classic literature and biographies.

Learning Materials

Along with books, libraries provide videos, magazines, computers, scanners and printers. Educational software is available. Look for discarded books to purchase. Ask when your library has its annual book sale. We have even had opportunity to attend special homeschoolers' events covering public speaking, crafts, favorite books, science and more.

✓ Foreign language or phonics tapes are available at some libraries. Do an intensive study while you have the program at home. Work until your child wants to stop. Start again after a break. Do as many sessions as possible, forgetting other subjects during this time. Then take the tapes back. Check the program out again in a week or two, and do another intensive study. If you are doing this with a very young child, make sure that he or she is ready for learning and that the program is enjoyable so that burn-out is avoided. Never push! More real progress will be made by letting your child set the pace.

Other Inexpensive or Free Resources

- For the cost of a stamp, you can write to your state government and ask about materials available for educators.
- Are there people in your community—friends or family—who have interesting lifestyles or careers? They might be willing to share their knowledge—perhaps even apprentice your child.
- What can you teach your children that you know? What would you like to learn with your child? Choose from balancing a checkbook, to gardening, to cooking, to any other specialized or ordinary talent that you have or want to learn!
- If you have a friend in a foreign country, ask him to try to find a penpal for your child. Our friend, Ali from Iran, couldn't find anyone who knew enough English but he did send us a wonderful photograph of ancient Persian ruins!
- Do you know of a foreign college student who would love sharing about his country while enjoying a home-cooked American meal and visit with you?

- Do you have encyclopedias? Teach from them! They are packed with information and if you have an old set, their content will be richer.
- Many free homeschool catalogs have teaching tips included with their product descriptions.
- Your local homeschool support group may have programs available for both you and your child. These will usually be free or low cost.
- Your child could be a volunteer at a living history museum.
- There are many free resources available online—books, courses, outline maps and worksheets. My favorite search engine is *www.google.com*.

✐ For teachers, the Internet can be quite helpful. For children, let the computer be a glorified typewriter—helping the words flow into wonderful prose. Let the Internet be the fantastic research tool that it is. However, because it is visual, limit time. If you want to accomplish really great things with your children, use books more than the computer.

Teacher Preparation

Good news! With EasyHomeschooling, teacher preparation is unnecessary—other than spiritual preparation and the occasional books you may wish to read. You save a lot of time. Instead of preparation for "classes," Mom learns along with the kids—as in reading aloud. Mom pursues other interests while the children work independently. I don't even keep a school log or diary, although many recommend it (and some states require it). It just seems like a waste of paper and time and I dislike clutter so I would probably throw it out eventually anyhow! Our children are the "journal" of their education. Once a year, you will design an annual teaching plan (scope and sequence) and a daily schedule. That's it! Then you are free to learn with your children each day. You *may* wish to keep a record of the great books that you read!

Workbooks and Texts

You may choose to use one or two purchased texts or workbooks. Used or antique are fine and less expensive—see "Enjoying Heirlooms," "Resources," or the Internet. These allow your child to work independently which is time-efficient. Some that we have used and can recommend are ☞ *Saxon* math for older students and *Learning Language Arts Through Literature. Bible Study Guide for all Ages* is a family study or all-grade study. It stresses the important doctrines and includes activities that the youngest child will enjoy.

It is very important to have a system of accountability for independent study and the use of workbooks. Check work daily—immediately is best, so that your child can have the satisfaction of having finished their day's work well. Don't allow sloppy work.

Don't forget, you are training for life!

Please don't go out immediately and buy suggested workbooks and texts! Read this whole book first and then you will be better able to decide just what you really need. Once you have made your decision to homeschool, God will equip you. He will provide whatever materials that you need and will give you novel ideas. A great blessing to me is how His timing is so perfect—such as the picture of ancient Persian ruins in Iran, sent by our friend during the time we were learning about ancient cultures! There were many other times when we saw God's provision for the topic or subject we were studying.

➥ As these blessings occur in your life, record them in your notebook. Reflecting on God's hand in your life can only increase your faith. You may also keep your day-to-day thoughts in a section labeled "Diary" or "Journal." You may see excerpts from my journals under the chapter headings in this book and an entire chapter covering several years of our homeschooling experiences in ❀ *Easy Homeschooling Companion,* "Drawing from my Diary."

The Basics and Excellency

Mastery—in the basic subjects of reading, writing and arithmetic—is the keystone of knowledge. These skills are used daily throughout life. In this book, I've shared the easy way to teach the basics. Although a large time investment is not needed to educate well, a concentrated focus during the time that you are schooling will multiply results.

Always follow up if your children are working independently. Drill math facts until they are known and known well. Do not allow calculator use. Require excellence. Attention to these and other suggestions will make the whole process much easier. Decide to be disciplined, even if you have to start with just one thing.

I know from experience how a school can just slide into inactivity, but it is always a mistake. If children know their honest best is expected and shoddy work is not accepted, they will not disappoint you. Be firm for a season and you will be blessed with diligent children who do excellent work.

Hurrah! You can forget about wasting time on such "subjects" as careers, communities and sex education. Instead of "Health," teach the Bible! *My son, attend to my words; incline thine ear unto my sayings. Let them not depart from thine eyes; keep them in the midst of thine heart. For they are life unto those that find them, and health to all their flesh* (Prov. 4:20-22).

Next you will learn how to free up more time for important activities by putting order into your home.

4
Making Order

Lord, what I need to do is overwhelming . . . I need a plan—a 1, 2, 3 list—a checklist and target dates. Let me know where to start, Lord, and order my steps. —September 9, 1998

A very undisciplined mom started our homeschool. I tore out paneling—and three years later we would be dining in a kitchen with unpainted plaster walls. I would spend hours—even days—looking through seed catalogs. I had never learned to work. Although my siblings had grown and left home—and I *should* have been helping more—my parents did everything. Interested in fashion, my pre-adult years were spent poring over fashion magazines. I carried many of these wasteful and irresponsible habits into my adulthood. I became bored quickly with employment, never keeping a job long. It was very difficult to stay motivated.

When we started schooling, we always had school regularly, but I accomplished little else. Since then I have learned to use lists, plans and schedules to save time and get us to our destination. In this chapter and the next I will explain the same procedures that have helped me fulfill many goals for myself and for our homeschool. You, too, will soon learn to draft your own blueprint for success!

Organizing Your Home

Our homes are havens for our homeschools. When home is in order schooling moves forward smoothly. We can make changes in this area in order to free time for homeschooling and for working toward other goals. If things aren't organized and accessible, we not only waste precious time searching, but our frustration at not finding the needed item(s) destroys the peace that should rule and reign.

Before starting our business, I organized everything in our house from files to sewing supplies. For years I kept my fabric in a large hinged box. Every time I would try to find something, I'd leave it in disorder. Then we purchased an old wardrobe at an auction, and my husband fitted it with shelves for fabric and notions. Shelves in a closet or even on a wall would work just as well. When you get organized, your frustrating moments will be fewer. We still have a few areas that get unorganized quickly but when I regularly clean and sort these, upkeep is not overwhelming.

The golden rule for making order out of chaos is to throw away, give away, put away. In one word—eliminate! Get rid of as much as you can do without. I love to see order emerging in this process. But I must confess, I have gone overboard in my quest for order and have later wished I had kept certain things—like depression glass, pink floral china, antique linens and our children's toys!

Steps to Order

1) Gather boxes for storage, and a broad-point marker for labeling. I like to use more boxes for trash so items can be easily tossed in. You could use paper grocery sacks or plastic trash bags. (Just make sure you do not accidently trash valuables! Always check the bags and boxes before disposing of them.) We sometimes used large plastic garbage "cans" and industrial laundry bins on wheels! They did not have to be emptied as often so were especially helpful in cleaning the second story of our home.

2) Throw away all obvious trash including papers, old mail and catalogs. You will see the beginnings of order and be inspired to continue with your task.

3) Work on one room at a time. As you sort and organize, you will find that you have items too good to toss, but that you neither want nor need. Put these items in separate boxes to give away or to sell at a garage sale. Label accordingly.

4) Box excess items that you can't bear to part with and label.

5) It is very important to put these "treasures" under lock and key, especially if you have young children who love to explore. Weeks of organizing can be destroyed in minutes by your bright, inquisitive children!

6) Go through all of your family's clothing, sorting as above. But this time have another pile for worn cotton garments. Cut these into one-foot squares for cleaning cloths. If you sew, you may wish to save the buttons from these clothes and reuse them. Use for cleaning, wiping up spills, washing cars, stripping woodwork and so forth. They not only save the cost of paper towels, they usually do a much better job!

7) My mother's maxim is a good one. "Have a place for everything and keep everything in its place." If you don't have a place, make a place.

Cleaning

Once your possessions are organized, you can begin cleaning. This might take a day—or even a month if you deep clean everything. I usually vacuum once a week, after having one or more of the children pick up. Children should have regular chores, such as keeping their rooms clean and neat, dusting, and washing dishes.

Major Cleaning

Choose a sunny day so you have lots of natural light. Unplug appliances before cleaning them and turn the electricity off at the breaker box before cleaning switches, outlets, and light fixtures. Your tools are a thick rough cloth or sponge, a bucket, warm or hot water, cleaner, a step ladder, an old dish brush, an old toothbrush and a larger floor scrub brush. The brushes will get into cracks, crevices, corners and embossed vinyl flooring. You could get by with one brush, such as the dish brush. Optional are protective gloves and goggles.

Tackle one room at a time. Kitchens and bathrooms take the most "elbow grease" so they are a good place to start. In the kitchen, it is best to do the insides of the cupboards, refrigerator and stove before the major cleaning. It might take a day to do the interiors, and another day to do the rest of the kitchen.

Do each room top to bottom starting with the ceiling. You may wish to use goggles to keep spatters out of your eyes. This cleaning strains lazy muscles, but I prefer washable ceilings. Each room does get easier! Clean the light fixture, then wash the upper walls, cupboards and lower walls. Windows can be done next.

Clean the floor thoroughly. I love my "ugly" Tri-Star® Compact canister vacuum because I can quickly take off the smooth floor attachment and use the metal tube to get into corners and along edges (and even along the ceiling with the brush attachment). Compacts are made well and do a good job, although very expensive if purchased new. When your floor is vacuumed (or swept), attack grime on hands and knees with a scrub brush and a strong cleaning solution. Do the baseboards at this time. Change the water often and rinse thoroughly if you want a truly clean floor. There are several all-purpose concentrated products available for washing smooth surfaces such as Mr. Clean,® Fantastic,® Simple Green® or a generic cleaner from a warehouse store like Sam's Club. A professional cleaning person says, "I use Super Clean® available from Wal-Mart in the auto section—strongest stuff you'll ever see—will take the skin off your fingers! It's in a gallon and will last a very long time. I dilute it about ten to one to clean almost everything . . . ."[1]

Give a final touch to your floor with a coat or two of wax. Before you know it your house will shine! To make cleaning more manageable, you may choose to do one major cleaning job each week or each month.

Once your home is clean and organized, simple daily and weekly upkeep will maintain it. To keep order, pick things up, or have your children pick things up immediately when that activity is finished. Have a ten minute daily "pick up" time before or after school. It really doesn't take long to keep your house in order. Letting it go is what makes the job overwhelming!

There are many books available to help with putting and keeping order in the home, such as those by Bonnie Runyan McCullough, Emilie Barnes, and ☞ **Don Aslett.**

I told them, "There's no fun like work!"

Delegate

The mutually beneficial relationship that family members share is seldom more evident than in the area of work. Working is a very, very important part of education, and one that is almost completely overlooked by schooling institutions. A phrase that I coined and use often with my children is: "There's no fun like work!" I love to work because I love to see the results of work—a clean house, a redecorated house, a weed-free garden, knowledgeable children, a quality product and so on. Our children make it possible for us to achieve much more than we could without them. But, our successes and accomplishments are their successes and accomplishments.

✗ Start early with each of your children, let them have some say in what they would like to do, enforce their choice until it becomes a habit and let them know you need them. Teach that *whatsoever a man soweth, that shall he also reap.* Tell them to *be not weary in well doing,* and to do their work *as to the Lord, and not unto men* (Gal. 6:7, 2 Thess. 3:13, Col. 3:23).

If you are financially able, pay your children for work well done *for the labourer is worthy of his hire* (Luke 10:7). Money does motivate, especially if your children are not already overly "blessed." But if you don't feel like you are able to pay them, fine! They are paid with food, clothing, shelter, occasional trips and treats.

Don't try to delegate to your husband. If he is working at a full time job, whatever he does around home is an additional blessing. Be thankful that he is supporting your family—many men aren't these days. Let your boys try the handyman jobs. Ezra, when nine, had already built a boat and a tool box and was quite handy and helpful, as was our youngest son Eli who even fixed a mower that the repair shop said couldn't be fixed!

Schoolroom

We began homeschooling informally so the whole world was our schoolroom. Our van was a schoolroom, as was the river and the back-yard. Our couch was our schoolroom, with babes on laps and cuddled nearby. This had to be one of life's most precious times. At that time our couch was directly in front of the bay windows, so we had lots of light. Next, we purchased our "teaching board" and wherever that happened to be was our schoolroom. We also used the dining room and kitchen tables.

Our first formal schoolroom was once a junk room. We made order in the room and it was beautiful, bright, spic and span. It was a pleasure to be there and conducive to learning. We decorated it with school things—our white board, a globe, maps and an antique wooden desk. One day the children and I went to an auction at an old school building and we picked up three more desks for one dollar each!

Next we moved upstairs to our large central hall and covered the walls with a time-line and a chart of the good and bad kings of Israel and Judah. When the hall was used for other purposes and the first schoolroom became an office, the desks spent some time in our

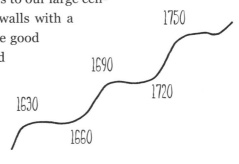

dining room with its floor-to-ceiling bookcase. Sunny bay windows and school decor completed the setting. I sometimes allowed the girls to take their individual studies up to their rooms. Later they all worked in their rooms at their desks. ☆ *It is very important to check progress often with this approach, unless you know duty has become a sure habit.*

As long as you do not neglect getting together for family read-aloud times, it really doesn't matter where you do school. I've just shared what we've done to show how flexible "location" can be. However, having a special room adds orderliness because everything is in one place. Time is spent on the important things and not wasted searching for something or moving from room to room. (If you school on your only table, you must clear it before meals.) It is also easier to supervise your children and their progress if they are in a special room with you, or working quietly while you tend to other things.

Now would be a good time to talk about those babies and toddlers—our solution was simple. We worked on school while they were napping. All of ours took long naps until they were about five or six. Older children can work independently while the little ones are awake.

✗ If possible choose a schoolroom with a southern exposure, especially if you live in a northern state.

✗ Get a low-cost white board from a building supply store. Ask for shower board.

Train them to nap if you have to!

5
Planning for Success

Planning and praying for our new school year . . . God's order and priorities . . . the best education possible. —July 6, 1994

I t may be that you struggle to stay motivated. Change for me was a process. Necessity was the catalyst that began that process. I learned procedures along the way that accelerated my ability to get more done in less time and motivated me to accomplish more. In Chapter 1, "Laying Foundations," the concept of recording dreams and goals was introduced. Now we will look into step lists, which are the key to meeting the goals you have set, which in turn will make your dreams come true.

Your Step List

➥ Open your notebook. If you haven't done so, make a separate list of your most important goals. You are now going to make a list of the steps you need to take to reach each of these goals. Start with your short-term goals because short-term goals are often steps to long term goals. For instance, one of my short-term goals is to get organized, which is also a step toward my long term goal of running a successful business. One of my step lists looks like this:

Goal: Become and Stay Organized

Today's Date_____

Date to be Accomplished_____

1) Get up earlier.
2) Stay up later.
3) Take a time inventory.
4) Make file folders as needed .
5) Sort and discard some clothing.
6) Put things back right after use.
7) Teach kids to do same.
8) Spend ten to fifteen minutes a day picking up.

•• Now list the steps that *you* will take to achieve each of your goals. The steps do not have to be in any particular order. At the left of each step write the date you begin to do it. Then when it becomes a habit or you have accomplished it, note that date on the right side and put one line through the step to cross it off, leaving it readable. It is encouraging to go back and see what you have achieved. You should have one page of steps for each goal. Each step may be simple or more complex—perhaps needing some steps of its own. Later we will detail another helpful tool—the monthly to-do list.

You can school anytime, or all of the time.

Homeschoolers can plan their school year for whatever suits them best. Some choose six weeks on, two weeks off year round. Others school year round with only a few days off. This schedule would make it possible for your child to be finished with his formal schooling at a much younger age or would enable you to spend less time per day on schoolwork. This would be an option for the teaching parent who works full time outside of the home. (See Chapter 12, "Building a Business" for more ideas on how to combine work and homeschooling.)

When our children were younger, I wanted to get outside first thing in the spring to garden. Living in the North, we all wanted to enjoy the warm seasons as much as possible, so we did most of our schooling in the winter when we had to be indoors anyway. I scheduled few hours for spring, summer and fall and many for winter. Our vacation ran from March or April to September or October, leaving only four or five months for intensive schooling. I knew that I would have to do some serious planning.

Scope and Sequence

"Scope" means *the area covered by a given activity* and "sequence" is defined as *the following of one thing after another.* Simply put, the scope and sequence shows what you plan to cover during your school year, and in what order. You can write your own scope and sequence in outline form with the main headings of language arts, mathematics, social studies (history, geography), health and science. Nebraska required a scope and sequence unless the parent-teacher used a standardized curriculum such as Abeka, Bob Jones or even the more flexible Robinson method. (See more on methods in Chapter 11, "Mining the Methods.") Drafting a scope and sequence may take a bit more effort once a year, but saves time and money throughout the year with better results. Even if your state does not require a scope and sequence, it would be a good idea to do one for your own benefit. You will be able to see at any point during the year what you have covered and what needs to be taught next.

✔ Begin school planning by viewing a curriculum guide such as the simplified ☞ *Course of Study* provided in back of this book. A course of study lists suggested topics for each grade. Pick and choose among topics for a grade level. Don't ever be enslaved by any course of study. If you would rather study a topic or subject that is not on the list, go ahead!

When I wrote my scope and sequence, I attempted to put some

order into into science and grouped similar topics together. One year we focused on botany, another on chemistry and so on.

In all subject areas, pick what you like from those listed. Look at the grades near your students' grades. If you have children in several different grades, you may combine topics or pick one that all can learn at the same time. I do this frequently with history, science and health. Teach your children who are close in age the same math and language arts. Look through several of the grades and plan ahead to achieve a continuity from year to year.

The following is an idea for a history plan. Again, this is an option only. Your plan will probably be much better! After covering these basics you could go on to English history or the history of another country. You could also study the history of missions, the history of the church, politics or law. Each number below is equivalent to a school year but not necessarily a school grade.

1) World history
2) American history
3) State history

Then, repeating in greater depth or with different emphasis

4) Egyptians, Greeks, Romans, Middle Ages
5) Renaissance and Reformation
6) American history: explorers to pioneers (including state history)
7) Pioneers to World War II
8) World War II to present

✔ After you have looked over the course of study, begin writing your ☞ **scope and sequence.** I have used the outline format most years. Other years I simply wrote a paragraph about what we were going to study under each subject heading. When writing an outline, your topic headings should be similar, and when using subtopics you should have at least two. For instance under your main heading, "Language Arts," you could have as subtopics, "Reading" and "Writing." Under "Writing" you could list "Themes" and "Poems." Or you could have all of the different language skills listed equally under your main topic. I often added the heading "Other," with "Music" and "Art" as subtopics. Then below each I listed what type or period of music or art we planned to cover. There may be other subjects or topics that you would like to teach your children. List them also. Make your scope and sequence as simple or as detailed as you like!

Times and Classes

After you have prepared your scope and sequence, you can begin writing your daily schedule. A schedule helps you stay on track and accomplish what needs to be done.

✔ Find the ☞ **Class Schedule Planner** in the back of the book. Enlarge and make several copies or write in pencil. Decide if you want to study a subject in the morning or afternoon. We almost always do Bible first—to honor God—and after that, math. It is usually best to do the more difficult subjects first. You may decide to do your "together" school—such as reading aloud—first, followed by individual studies such as math. The younger students usually are done before the older ones, so the older ones could continue working on their own after lunch. You can also spend whole days, a week or even a month on one subject or topic. You are the designer! But do plan and schedule, for progress can be haphazard without a plan, just as getting to a destination is often difficult without a road map.

You are the designer of your family school.

To find out how many pages of a workbook or text that your child should do each day:
1) Count the pages or chapters. How many total days do you plan to do school? Let's say your school year is 9 months. Each month has 4 weeks. You have decided to school for 5 days of each week.
2) Multiply to find our how many total days you will be schooling. First multiply 9 times 4 to get a total of 36 weeks. Then multiply 36 x 5 days per week to arrive at 180 days. Your child's penman-

ship book has 200 pages.

3) Divide 200 by 180 to get 1.11 pages per day. Have your student do one and one half pages per day, which would allow for an occasional missed day. Toward the end of the year, readjust the daily work, perhaps cutting back to one page a day. (Divide the number of pages left by the number of days left.) If 180 days of school are planned and there are only 72 pages in a text, you will know that book or subject will only have to be done about 2 times a week. If you find that your child needs to do a subject twice a week, choose the days—say Tuesday and Thursday—and enter the subject under those days in the proper time slot. (Science and health are often done only twice a week.)

After you have written a school schedule a few times, it will be easy. Pray first! Then fill out your planning sheet with whatever times, subjects and intervals you want. You may want to write a note at the bottom or side. I started my chart at 5:00 a.m. one year, because I wanted to list all activities upon arising, such as quiet time and chores.

Your schedule is a tool to help you get more learning done in less time. It is not your master but your slave. Do *not* use it as a weapon. You could use Gayle Graham's idea in *How to Homeschool* and have an alternate schedule for the days you need to stay in bed a little longer. That way you won't be tempted to forget schooling completely on that day. Informal learning—such as reading aloud, library trips, vacations, field trips or other outings—can also be counted as time spent on schooling, so don't fret if you have not spent as much time on task as your schedule says you should.

The Monthly To-Do List

➦ Look at your step lists and from that make another list. This list will be your monthly to-do list. Only put as much on it as you think can reasonably be accomplished. I have fourteen entries on one month's list. These are things that you will be working on almost every day of the month. These are the most important activities that will bring you the results you want for your life, your children and your family.

If there is something on your list that you do not have completed at the end of the month, transfer that to the next month's list if it is still a priority. When things become routine, it is not necessary to list them. Your list is for projects unique to each day, month, step and goal. Usually your monthly to-do list and your daily list—if you have one—will list an assortment of activities relating to many steps and goals. Here is one of my monthly to-do lists:

1) Send letter & tracts to residents of my town.
2) Start book. Write one chapter.
3) Cover letter to publisher.
4) Learn graphics.
5) Study and apply marketing tools.
6) Make dresses for girls.
7) Write article.
8) Compile media data.
9) Query letter for article.

It is also a good idea to note the date when each activity is accomplished. By regular use of your step list and monthly list you will be spending most of your time on the priorities which will move you toward your goals and dreams.

➡ You can even break your monthly list down into smaller steps. Mary Kay called this her "$35,000 List." Each night, she made a list of ten things to accomplish the next day.[1]

You can do this too. Look at your monthly to-do list, and make yet another list of about six things to do the following day. (If your list is a short one, it is more likely that you will complete it.) This is called the $35,000 List because that's what the president of a large company paid a professional organizer after his staff increased business profits by more than $35,000 after beginning this simple technique.

Spend your time on what matters most!

Motivation for Children

After you have learned how to set goals, and have met a number of them, you are qualified to teach this tremendous motivational system to your older children. Give them a permanent notebook with dividers and have them start with their dreams, just as you did. Let them spend a few days or weeks praying about, and then compiling their dream list. Then go on and teach them about goals. A goal is a desired effect that can be met within a period of time. Then teach them to compose their goal lists, step lists, monthly lists and daily to-do lists. Emphasize that this is a lifetime project and that their notebook needs to be updated regularly. You may choose to have a "notebook day" once a month until this becomes habitual. As your children see what steps they need to take to meet their goals—and see the progress made by completing these steps—they will take responsibility upon themselves. They will discover that personal initiative produces the results that they want for their lives—just as it does for us. *Commit thy works unto the LORD, and thy thoughts shall be established* (Prov. 16:3).

Have a "notebook day" once a month.

6
Combining Subjects

The girls are doing reports on the astronomers, Copernicus and DaVinci. —May 8, 1995

Have you ever washed dishes while cooking or read while eating? If you have, you have combined tasks. You can also combine subjects to make the most of the time you spend at homeschooling. The following are suggested activities. We did them over several years. Do not try to tackle them all at once. Never neglect the basics to clutter the curriculum with any added activities. The greatest portion of schooling time should be spent reading aloud, and—as your children mature—reading silently.

History

"History is a voice forever sounding across the centuries the laws of right and wrong . . . ."[1] Following the history plan from your scope and sequence (last chapter) or the table of contents from a text, choose books to read aloud. To save money, use your library. We used books from the children's section to introduce a period or country. Historical novels and biographies are even better choices. Your reading will lead to people or events that you will wish to learn

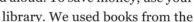

more about. Then you can get additional biographies and other more exhaustive books. Combine history with language arts, fine arts, penmanship, home economics, science, travel, geography, Bible and speech.

Language Arts

- Dictate some of the more memorable passages from your reading. (See upcoming section on spelling for instructions.)
- Have your children research a particular aspect of history or a person and write a paper.

Penmanship

- Read history (or science) while your children are doing penmanship or a detailed art lesson. Borrow art videos and other materials about the period you are studying from your public library or from the ☞ **National Gallery of Art.** Purchase inexpensive project booklets on different periods of history from ☞ **Kids Art.** While children are working on art projects, read biographies of artists from the period you are studying.

Fine Arts

- Create a timeline. Get ends of newsprint rolls from your local newspaper. Draw a wavy horizontal line with a wide marker. Label each hill and valley with a year 30 years apart (1630, 1660, etc.), leaving enough space for the events of those thirty years (about 18-24 inches). Have your children draw a picture of each historical figure or event studied with colored markers, including the date of his or her life, or date of event. (Shown is a greatly reduced sample; it was not at an angle.) Ours was very long and we had to put it up along our tall ceilings and over the tops of some doorways. Later we rolled it up for storage.
- ✐ Another timeline idea is to use a notebook. Place punched construction paper or poster board into a three-ring binder. Paste

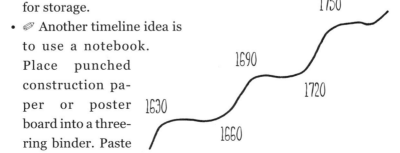

pictures cut from magazines, or have your student draw a person or an event from that period and label. You could put each event on one page, with the date at the top of the page, and then put them in order, or you could have one page for each decade. Yes, have your children memorize the most important events and dates.

- ✐ Although the above idea is easier to work with, it does not show the full span of history. Perhaps you could do the actual timeline as in the first suggestion, only cutting the time periods into centuries or other divisions so that your timeline is not so long. Then occasionally you could lay it out end to end if you could find room, even outside in the summer on a windless day.

Home Economics

- I have crocheted gift afghans while my girls read, and later they crocheted afghans while I read. You could knit, do needlepoint, embroider or even hem garments during this time.
- ✐ One capable child could be cooking or baking while you read.
- ✐ You could do crafts from the period, especially valuable home-making or building crafts.

Science

- When studying a period of history, you can veer into scientific topics or personalities. We have done this during our Renaissance study by combining science concepts and the astronomers, da Vinci and Galileo. Your older children could do research and then write a paper.

Travel

- Visit historical sites. Have your children journal about what they have learned. Take photographs or do sketches for a scrapbook to be completed at home. (Scrapbooking is a ☞ **Cindy Rushton** learning idea.)

Geography

- Always look up the place that you are learning about on a map or globe.

Bible

- Study Bible history to learn God's will and His ways along with ancient and creation history.

Speech

- Speech skills can be practiced reciting memorized Bible verses.
- Have your children read history aloud, practicing the speech skills of enunciation, projection, emphasis and pronunciation.
- Speeches and historical documents—such as the *Gettysburg Address*—can be memorized. Take several days or even weeks to memorize longer passages.

How to Memorize

1) Read the complete work together several times.
2) Recite the first sentence together several times.
3) Add another sentence as soon as the first is committed to memory—always reciting all that is known, from the beginning.
4) When you are able to say the entire piece together from memory, start testing your children individually.
5) Once learned, practice often (overlearn), lest it be forgotten.

State History

You can study your state's history using the same combinations mentioned above with free and low-cost materials. Begin planning by contacting your state's government offices. This time, some of those tax dollars will benefit you! Write or call these offices that often have free information or materials.

- Tourism
- Economic Development
- Natural Resources
- Game (wildlife) and Parks
- Historical Society

The Department of Tourism will have an attractive thick "magazine" that will provide background information, including historical sites and other interesting tidbits. General books about your state, from your library, can be used as an introduction to this study. Read them with your children. Then choose specific areas to focus on. What would you like to know more about? Does your child show an interest in a particular topic? Our boys love to "rough" it and were interested in explorers and cowboys. You might choose native residents, immigrants, exploration or geography. Here is a list of the free or low-cost materials that we used in our state study:

- A booklet of quotes about Crazy Horse. (Native Americans had wonderful memories because their minds were their journals!)
- A man's overview of Nebraska published by the Economic Development Department.
- A booklet describing a particular fort and the daily routines there.
- A free publication called "Trail Tales" published by Game and Parks that features articles on wildlife, endangered species, land areas, nature study and making bird feeders.
- A free newspaper from the historical society. I actually got to pick topics for the six issues and each child received a personal copy.

Combine state history with literature, science, nature study, cultures, the arts, language arts and geography.

Literature

- I wanted to focus on our state's literary heritage, so we read some of our best authors, such as Willa Cather (*My Antonía, O Pioneers!*). Parts of the television version of *My Antonía* were filmed just a few miles from our home. Our living history museum—where more of the movie was filmed—offered a free premiere showing to local residents.

Science

- Although a state study may have history for its hub, other subjects can studied at the same time. We took a scientific field trip to a dig site in our state. This stimulated a discussion about how those bones actually got there and how the Great Flood may have played a part. We saw wrong and speculative information set forth as fact, notified the paleontologist in writing and received a response.

Nature Study, Cultures, The Arts

- Does your coastal state have a large aquarium or other zoo? Is there a special culture native to your area that you could study? (Spaniards in California, French in Louisiana, etc.) Has a former or current resident done something notable in art or music?

Many populated areas are resource-rich in the arts. Take advantage of this!

Language Arts

- As soon as possible after your field trip, have your child write about the outing, telling what they have learned about their state.

Geography

- Give your children a map while traveling and let them mark your route. Study counties before you go. Passing through the actual area will make the map and the names come alive. Have them draw a map of your state and label each county after they have memorized them. You can also do this with states, or even countries if you are a world traveler or a European citizen. ✐ You could use free outline maps from the Internet for this.

A state study can be as open-ended or as focused as you desire. Make it personal and enjoy the time with your family. Mini-vacations visiting your state's sites will foster family togetherness. One of our most memorable state field trips was visiting Chimney Rock and Scottsbluff National Monument, a pioneer passage west. God broke the clouds directly over the cliff-like rock formation and brought along a once-in-a-lifetime centennial pony-express rider soon after we arrived!

Spelling

If you start reading aloud to your children when young, following the suggestions in Chapter 2—teaching one thing at   a

time and giving your children plenty of opportunity to experience many good books, spelling will not have to be taught. Zephi taught herself to read at five and also taught herself to spell. Seeing an abundance of the printed word, she observed and assimilated proper spelling. Jessica didn't spell quite as well, but she also did not read as well or as much. When I suggested that Jessica become more attentive to how words were spelled in her reading, her spelling also improved. Our sons have always needed more help. Because of the research done by ☞ **Dr. Raymond Moore** suggesting that boys mature later than girls, and my own tendency to baby our "babies," I did not expect as much from them. The result was that they did not read as early, nor spell as well ✐ and spelling class has continued up through high school!

Mama, help those babies grow up.

Phonics
- If you are going to teach spelling, the perfect time is at the same time you teach phonics because phonics rules are spelling rules!
- A book such as ☞ ***Simply Phonics*** is ideal because it lists the words in families with like sounds and spellings. During each phonics lesson, encourage your child to pay attention to what letters make up each word. Afterwards test orally (or in writing, if they can write). *Simply Phonics* could also be used with an older child who is having difficulty with spelling.

Language Arts
- Copying (copywork) from the Bible or classic literature is an excellent way to learn language arts, including spelling. Your student reads the selection and copies it. This is easy on the teacher because the proper grammar forms, punctuation, capitalization and spelling are in the selection. Dictation is another effective learning technique. Here's how:

Dictation

1) Let your students spend some time studying the passage.
2) Read the piece as slowly as necessary for them to get it down.
3) Older children now check (proofread) and edit, marking any errors they think they might have.
4) Teacher checks for grammar, punctuation and spelling mistakes.
5) Make a separate list of misspelled words to look up and correct. (If your children are younger, write the correct spelling for them to learn.)
6) Have your student write each misspelled word about ten times each or speak the spelling aloud.
7) Finally, give an oral or written test.

If your child needs review, he will misspell the word again (and then you will go through the above steps again). To avoid extra work, he will try harder to spell more words correctly and will either learn the words, or look them up. To discover what grade level your child is at in spelling, you can test occasionally using *A Measuring Scale for Ability in Spelling.* ✐ Get from www.amazon.com. You can also use this for spelling lists, if you decide you want your child to learn the most commonly used words.

At least once a week, besides your dictation work, your children should write a story, or other piece. Make sure it's not too long for your younger students. If they are reading independently, they can write about what they have read (this is ideal). Then go on to correct and make a spelling list according to the directions given above for copying and dictation. It is important that your children learn neatness, so it is best that their papers be done in pencil. Otherwise they will have to recopy.

Geography

Combine with research, missions, games, literature and history.

Research, Missions

- Make your own calendar or plan, listing one country a week. After checking what country is listed on the calendar for that day, find it on the globe and pray for the people there. Have your children do research and report on that country after pointing it out on a world map or globe.

Games

- Play games such as "Where in the World" or "Take Off."

Literature

- Read books such as *Hans Brinker* (The Netherlands) or *Treasures of the Snow* (Switzerland). ✐ *All Through The Ages* lists books by time periods and geographic regions.

Current Events

- An event in the news can spark a mini-study on a country and its geography.

History

- Geography will be related to historical studies. While studying English history read about England, Ireland, Scotland and Wales. Always find the country that you are reading about on a globe.

Math

Focused Attention

It is so important that parents give their children focused attention. This does not always come easily, even for homeschoolers. Math "class," especially for younger students, is an excellent time for giving this focused attention. Put the baby down for a nap, and send the other children off to work on their own while you spend special time with one of your children. I don't know if I've ever felt closer to our youngest! His smiling brown eyes looked into mine, wondering if his answer was correct. Remember, when it takes a little more time to get them to understand, instead of getting frustrated and short tempered, demonstrate patience and let this be a special time. And be sure to praise them when they get it right!

Speech

- Do oral math with your children. Have them speak the problem and solution in complete sentences and with proper diction.

Nature Study

"I love to think of nature as an unlimited broadcasting station through which God speaks to us every hour, if we will only tune in . . . "[2]

Family Time

Many of us live in beautiful locations where free educational opportunities abound. We spend many pleasant hours in the summer on the sand bars at our river or going on country drives. More than once we have had wonderful nature sightings—deer, bald eagles, hawks, even panther paw prints! Our children certainly can identify more than I could when I was their age! This is an example of learning along with your children.

Drawing, Crafts

- Go outside, open your eyes and *see!*
- Get your children sketchbooks. Sit in a secluded spot (one child at a time works best) and let the richness of creation pour in. Whenever you go on an outing, have a sketching time as part of that outing. Art school students are never without their sketchbooks!
- Check with your state Game and Parks Commission for nature guides for your locality and use them to identify plants and animals.
- Sketch what you are seeing. (Drawing instructions coming later in the book).
- Label your drawings.

Literature, Language Arts

- Read books like those by Ernest Thompson Seton.
- Have your children keep a nature diary as did the naturalist and writer, John Burroughs.

✔ To make a simple plaster model of animal prints, cut a strip of poster board or other cardboard about one and one-half inches by one foot (depending on size of print). Form it into a ring, and paper-clip together. Push the ring into the soil around the animal print. Mix plaster of Paris according to the directions and pour into the cardboard ring that you have pushed in the soil.

Combining Students

Have older children be responsible for tutoring a sibling. Our youngest son didn't want to begin his first *Saxon* text with me or our eldest daughter. But as soon as twelve-year-old Zephi took over, he did three pages! Even if your older child is not particularly gifted, tutoring will help develop their patience and personal skills.

Other Combinations

- Combine vacations with studies by reading about deserts (mountains, the seashore, etc.) before visiting that area and that area's museums.
- Study artists and art history before visiting art museums.
- Study local history and spend a lot of time at local museums.

Our girls attended "school" in an 1890s one-room schoolhouse at our living museum. (This is where I noticed that they were reading better than other homeschoolers their age.)

We have fond recollections of the Civil War re-enactment near "Railroad Town." What beautiful period music, clothing and dancing we savored that balmy summer night! Yet—and importantly—our background reading made it bittersweet, knowing the very real suffering that families experienced during that time.

Now It's Your Turn!

➥ As you homeschool, you will discover your very own combinations that will save time and make homeschooling easier and more enjoyable! Again, you may choose to write these ideas in your notebook.

7
Enjoying Heirlooms

Thank you Lord! I am so pleased with the boys' writing—they are already using high quality literary terms. Could part of it be their use of the KJV for such a long time? —September 18, 1998

Growing up in a modern 1950s house with its sterile decor left me reaching back for something fuller and richer. My father worked in a museum and I almost hated to visit—I didn't just want to look at the treasures, I wanted to own them!

Today our priority in dress seems to be comfort whereas in the past it was appearance, including cleanliness, neatness and presentability before God and others. Even as recently as the 40s, 50s and into the 60s women wore hats when they did simple activities such as shopping. How wonderfully the Victorians dressed themselves and their houses. Even my grandmother had a beautiful wedding dress— and she lived on the prairie.

Precious People

God gives a great treasure in precious older ones. One blessing is that they can share a tremendous amount of history, because they lived it! I am so thankful that our children had a chance to know their grandparents. When we were studying our community, our then seven-year-old daughter interviewed her grandmother. She found out that her great-grandfather was the first rural mail carrier in our area. Later we saw a picture of his "box" on wheels with "U.S. Mail" on the side and a small square opening in front for the reins to pass thorough—keeping out the cold winter winds. Mom told us how he had come to America alone, lived with an uncle for a time and then traveled on to Nebraska.

My father's family lived over the hills in another small community. Uncle Theo, Dad's oldest brother, told how Grandma would bathe, hitch the horses to the buggy and ride over here through the dusty hills. Because she was expecting my father, she came to see Dr. Dickinson, who built, lived in and had his office in the house we have called home for nearly twenty-five years. My two oldest uncles would play on our lawn. How could history be more interesting!

One of our town's oldest residents also shared local history. He's told us about the charm of our tiny community when it was a boom "railroad" town with livery stables and blacksmith shops. He even told us about incidents in his grandmother's life. When she was a child, the Indians ransacked their cabin. The motive for this incident became apparent as we read about the Indians' very real hunger as natural game was depleted.

✔ Ask your older friends and relatives to tell you or your child about their life when they were younger. General facts can be remembered, but you may want to jot down names and locations. Have your child do a written or oral report after the interview.

"What did you do when you were my age?"

In our studies, we found out that my great-great-grandfather (1829-1924) "had a brilliant mind and at one time was one of the largest landholders in Sherman County"[1] He and his son (1856-1941) came to Nebraska in a covered wagon, taking over a month to get here from Illinois. Great-Great-Grandfather enjoyed splitting wood up to his death at age ninety-six. My mother-in-law said that her grandfather was from Persia (Iran). Even today, there are only a handful of immigrants from the Middle East in our whole state. Those who settled here came from Sweden, Denmark, Germany, Poland, Czechoslovakia and Bohemia.

You too can discover interesting tidbits on your family tree! Visit with family. Check the public library for basic books. Make friends with your reference librarian. Search the Internet. Just as historical studies lead into deeper and deeper studies, genealogical studies can do the same and may become a lifetime hobby.

Skills and Ministry

Older people have had years to develop skills. Perhaps they could teach your child something that they do well. How about bartering some home cooked meals for these "classes"? You would meet a primary need for some of these older people! Let your children help in food preparation. Andy's co-worker could not believe that our little girl had made the bread that he was eating for lunch, nor could he believe that she had been doing it for years. These are skills that other children may not learn until they are adults—I didn't! Homeschooling trains for life.

✔ For a ministry and history project, adopt a nursing home and go from resident to resident visiting and questioning them about their past. Perhaps you could talk with one resident each visit. Compile your notes into a "book"—each chapter about an individual resident. Most residents have lots of time—but little to do—and would love the company.

Another way to bless those dear ones in care homes, as well as improving musical talents is to learn *a capella* harmonizing. Get tapes from ☞ *The Lester Family.* On the tapes, the parts are sung separately so they can be learned, and then all parts are sung together. Beautiful!

Heirloom Books

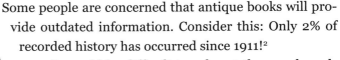

Some people are concerned that antique books will provide outdated information. Consider this: Only 2% of recorded history has occurred since 1911![2]

It would be difficult to exhaust the core knowledge found in older books, no matter what the subject. I've found that older books cover the most important topics and ideas more thoroughly and clearly.

To be classified as an antique, an item should be at least fifty years old. In our area, it would be difficult to find a book at a reasonable price and in good condition with a date before 1860. This may be because our state was settled around that time and only a few books were brought with the pioneers. Those that were transported were probably Bibles and copies of *Pilgrim's Progress* that were very used and subsequently worn out before my grandparents were born.

I prefer books with a copyright date from around 1860 to 1930, although newer books with copyright dates into the late 40s can also be delightful. Some books published in the 50s might be acceptable—but not *Dick and Jane* sight readers. Not all books published between these optimal dates are worth buying but they are generally far superior to what you would find today. Another option is to purchase reprinted books such as the ☞ 1879 *McGuffey* readers, available from ☞ **Home School Treasures.** Little Bear Wheeler of ☞ **Mantle Ministries** also reprints some wonderful old books.

In addition to our inventory of ☞ **Exceptional Books,** we have a personal library of old books—acquired throughout the years. When our children were younger, my husband would make a weekly stop at a small library to pick up these "keepers" that the librarian replaced with newer (and often inferior) titles. Some that we acquired during that time were *Kidnapped, The Black Arrow, The Works of Shakespeare, Les Miserables, Treasure Island* and *Little House on the Prairie.*

88

✘ Look for low-cost, old books at your local thrift store. Several years ago we found an oversized well-written devotional book with a 1936 copyright. This beautiful book was garnished with photos, drawings, stories, poems and scriptures—and in great condition! We have also purchased Bibles and Bible teaching tapes from thrift stores. We found special books at garage sales—such as a poetry book that I had been wanting for years. Auctioneers gave us boxes of books that didn't sell. Even now we occasionally hear of a large number of books that have been trashed because no takers were found. With prayer, you can be in the right place at the right time. Check with your relatives. Search attics. Buy lower-cost, paperback reprints. Soon you will be able to use the books that you have collected and avoid annual homeschooling expenses and trips to the library, while your children thrive.

There are two basic categories of antique books for the homeschooler—the classic novel and the textbook. The classic novel is sometimes available as an unabridged reprint—but be careful! Some "unabridged" reprints are not the original text, so choose the oldest book you can find rather than a newer copy, whenever possible.

Develop a taste for vintage books.

The antique textbook is not as readily available as a reprint, yet is a valuable tool. In this category you will find history texts; historical, literary and nature readers; Latin dictionaries and math books.

Other categories are children's novels, biographies and non-fiction. We have an antique set of *The Book of Knowledge* encyclopedias. It is so rich in history, authors, literature, poetry and more, it could be used, along with a Bible, for your entire curriculum. It even includes a study-guide volume.

For Preschool and Elementary

Do not hesitate to use classic novels to read aloud to your youngest child. Many classics have interesting story lines that your children will follow, especially if yours is a TV- and video-free home. There are books of shorter devotions or moral stories that would also be appropriate for this age.

Continue reading aloud to your elementary-age children. Read aloud from all antique books—your *King James Bible,* history and science textbooks, classic novels, and so forth. Discuss or have your children write about what has been read. Once you start reading aloud, one thing will lead to another. When you find yourself liking a particular poet, look up his biography. Find the author's homeland, state or city on the globe. Then read a book about that place.

Arithmetic

Antique textbooks were written for a child to use and understand so the teacher should have no problem! Many of them include explanatory prefaces and introductions along with answers. They provide problems for young children that are simple enough to check quickly. With the more advanced texts, answers will certainly save time, but you can also use a calculator or have an older child use a calculator or his brain (preferred) to check the work. Teach your children to do exercises very carefully and to always double-check their answers. You may choose to have your child do just a few of the problems presented. This would certainly make checking easier but make sure that he or she is getting enough practice to be learning.

After two or three years of using ☞ *Practical Arithmetics*, I found that the *Saxon* books were about two levels behind our daughters. We made copies of the pages from the old book and the girls used them like worksheets. The numbers were quite small but they did their figuring on another sheet. Traditionally, the complete problem was copied onto a blackboard or onto notebook paper. You can enlarge the page when you copy it, to use it as a worksheet.

Language Arts

Selections from old poetry books can be memorized and recited. Dictate from them to teach grammar and spelling. Dictate short selections from classic fiction. Dictation is described in detail in Chapter 6, "Combining Subjects," under the heading, "Spelling."

After learning to read, our children used *McGuffey's*, the reprinted readers. In the second grade, the girls were at fourth-grade level according to the teacher's guide. I simply had them read to me every day, one lesson at a time. We ignored all the other suggested activities.

History

Use an old history text's table of contents for a guide for the history section of your scope and sequence. Read books written at that period of time by someone who lived then, or about that time. If you are introduced to a person you would like to know more about, get a biography from the public library, your personal library or other book source. Do related activities such as studying the art of that period, and even attempting to re-create it. Listen to the music of that epoch in history.

Prepare to experience vibrant history.

Science

You can do similar studies with science and scientists. Collect scientific biographies, texts, literary works and old experiment books. Combine a biography with books on that scientist's field of research. Re-create his experiment. Write and report.

Bible

The KJV Bible is an antique book that will never be outdated. Along with its great spiritual weight, it is an outstanding literary work and example of proper English. It has no equal among the newer versions and should be a major part of the Christian's homeschool.

Avis graduated from 8th grade when 11!

Find someone who was educated with these books. Ask the person what they learned in school. You will be amazed at what many of them still remember after fifty or sixty years! A psychiatrist who evaluated my mother's memory loss said that her spelling and writing were impeccable for a woman her age. Of course he was a young "whipper-snapper" who didn't consider that most older people were better educated than even he, with his many degrees.

In 1907, Avis Carlson received her eighth-grade diploma. Later in life, she found her examination questions and was surprised at their difficulty: "The questions on that examination in that primitive one-room school, taught by a person who never attended a high school, positively dazed me."[3] Avis was only eleven years old when she exhibited proficiency that today would be beyond exceptional.

1907 Education
Home and Health, © 1907, Pacific Press Publishing

> *A child is recognized as well-educated if he can read distinctly and intelligently, spell correctly, write a smooth, plain hand; and if he acquires a knowledge of the fundamental rules of arithmetic, a fairly good knowledge of the geography of the world and the history of his own country. But if he acquires all the languages, arts and sciences of the schools, without a knowledge of the fundamentals above mentioned, he will forever be set down as an ignorant man.*

In selecting a child's reading material, the line should be drawn between the good and the bad. A serious mistake is often made by separating arbitrarily between truth and fiction. Much that is true in this wicked world is the most debasing; while some imaginative incidents, stories and allegories are the most elevating and beneficial. Parents should select the reading for their children with the utmost care. The contents of every book read should be known to parents. Liberal enough provision should be made to keep the children interested in the reading planned for them, so that the active little minds will not reach out with a hungry longing for the worthless story books of their playmates. This mental chaff and rubbish will sooner or later prey upon their morals.

One of the most certain ways by which children are led to novel reading is by the negative system of controlling their reading. They are positively forbidden even to look at books of a certain class, but at the same time nothing is provided to satisfy the honest literary hunger of their little hearts. Under such restrictions, children too often secure bad books and read "on the sly," and really go to injurious lengths, far beyond where their unrestrained desires would have led them.

In this evil world, sin is made most enticing. Bad books are often more fascinating than good ones and the unguided child is almost certain to choose them. As soon as the child can begin to comprehend and appreciate what is read to him, he should be led into the most interesting and beneficial literary treasures which can be provided for him. Then when his taste is developed so that he can appreciate and enjoy the good, the true and the beautiful, he will have a bulwark of good taste and principles built up around him, which will naturally shut him out from much of the world's sin and folly.

See Chapter 13, "Sailing Through High School," to find out how to use antique books for high schoolers.

8
Training for Eternity

Lord, help me to know what to do day by day, moment by moment, to train them in the Way—in your wisdom. —January 3, 1989

Just as Noah prepared the ark for the saving of his house, when you commit to Christian homeschooling you begin construction on your family's ark. The ark is the strong spiritual foundation that your children will take with them when they emerge from your loving embrace. They will then be equipped to please God, having learned what He requires. *But without faith it is impossible to please him: for he that cometh to God must believe that he is, and that he is a rewarder of them that diligently seek him* (Heb. 11:6). This foundation of faith will enable your children to face, repel and overcome every storm that attempts to come against them in their lives.

Three Keys to Success

 There are three keys to raising children to be godly young adults. These are not secrets. The difficulty is in the doing. The keys, in order of difficulty, are:

1) Modeling God's ways (being the example)
2) Praying in faith for your children
3) Giving God's Word its proper place

Modeling

I consider modeling most important, as well as most difficult. We have to know the Word to portray it, but even in cultures and creeds where God's Word is not known, ☆ *children grow into what their parents have modeled.* This is a tremendous responsibility! Even if we haven't measured up to the task previously, we can start now to be the parents that we should be. We are told in Philippians 3:13 to *forget those things which are behind, and reach forth unto those things which are before.*

Praying in Faith

The next key to having godly children is praying in faith. Don't just take it for granted that your children will turn out okay. Don't pray haphazardly. Pray specifically for their godliness and devotion to Jesus, even naming particular qualities or needful areas. In an old issue of *An Encouraging Word,* Vickilynn Haycraft tells about the Jewish custom of praying for each child's spiritual well-being while making challah on Friday, in preparation for the special Sabbath meal. You could pray for your children daily while preparing meals.

Part two of praying in faith is believing that Faithful God has heard and answered the prayer, even if the results aren't immediately seen with physical eyes. God never fails if we don't let our faith fail. *Therefore I say unto you, What things soever ye desire, when ye pray, believe that ye receive them, and ye shall have them* (Mark 11:24). If your children seem to be missing the mark, remember *we walk by faith, not by sight* (2 Cor. 5:7). *And let us not be weary in well doing: for in due season we shall reap, if we faint not* (Gal. 6:9).

Giving God's Word Its Proper Place

We need to give God's Word its rightful place in our homes. God has *magnified His Word even above His name* (Ps. 138:2). The Word will teach the work ethic, wisdom, spiritual warfare, how to pray and a disposition to be generous or helpful. It will give freedom from quarrels and disagreement. It will provide guidance regarding life ministry and career, and provide *all things that pertain unto life and godliness* (2 Pet. 1:3). The most marked change in our children's behavior has been after we seriously studied a section of Scripture such as 2 Peter 1:5-10.

We are not modeling the fear of the Lord when we ignore God's Word while spending most of our time doing other things. I've often thought how much greater our growth and fruits would be if we had no other books, magazines or printed material in our home. But how do we start now? We cannot do it on our own. *I can do all things through Christ which strengtheneth me* (Phil. 4:13). We start with just one thing as Clay and Sally Clarkson suggest in their book *Educating the WholeHearted Child.*

The King James Bible

There is no equal to the *Authorized King James Version* of the Bible. It has been called "the noblest monument of English prose."[1] The other versions are dumbed down, yet actually more difficult to understand. Here's why the KJV is better for your children. If—after reading this— you still feel that you must use another version, go right ahead. It is better to use some Bible rather than no Bible!

- New versions give your children a model of poor writing with grammatical and style mistakes.
- Flesch-Kincaid's grade level indicator ranks the KJV easier to read in 23 out of 26 comparisons because of the KJV's use of one and two syllable words and simple sentence structure.
- Second grade students can define several KJV words but few in the NKJV.
- The one word that may not be familiar in the KJV is actually more precise than its replacement.
- Newer versions use twice the number of words and syllables to say the same thing and yet the NIV has 64,000 fewer words, because whole sections have been left out![2]

Teaching the Bible

All scripture is given by inspiration of God, and is profitable for doctrine, for reproof, for correction, for instruction in righteousness (Tim. 3:16). *And thou shalt teach them ordinances and laws, and shalt show them the way wherein they must walk, and the work that they must do* (Ex. 18:20).

There is no doubt about it. God's Word is to be our curriculum. It is much too complete to add to. The only commentator should be the parent—submissive to and guided by the Holy Spirit. *And thou shalt teach them diligently unto thy children, and shalt talk of them when thou sittest in thine house, and when thou walkest by the way, and when thou liest down, and when thou risest up* (Deut. 6:7). If your children say that you should be a preacher, you are doing things right! ✐ However, you should *not* be condemning and harsh in your "preaching."

The Bible will change character faster than all the character training books or manuals put together! Why? It is *God's* Word—*quick, and powerful, and sharper than any two-edged sword, piercing even to the dividing asunder of soul and spirit, and of the joints and marrow, and is a discerner of the thoughts and intents of the heart* (Heb. 4:12).

Technique

✔ For learning and teaching the Bible use a dictionary. To use the Bible's self-contained dictionary (looking at a word in several different verses), you will also need a concordance. If you haven't studied the Word in this way, you will be amazed at the spiritual insight you will receive when using these simple tools.

All should have their own KJV Bible and follow along while the Word is read. It is ideal for the parent to read at this time because he or she is able to pause at the Spirit's leading for discussion. Although you may wish to share reading, different skill levels may hinder the focus of this class. In our home, if the reading has not been done well, I will reread the verse as we discuss it.

Another option is listening to Bible tapes while all follow along. The parent can run the tape player and pause when desired. Of course, if your children want to comment or initiate discussion during listening or reading, that should be allowed and encouraged.

To dig deeper, try the following techniques. We drafted these charts and diagrams on our "teaching" or dry-erase board. List natural divisions, repeated words, contrasts or comparisons.[3]

✔ If it looks like there is a list of similar words, or if the passage can be outlined, do that. Unknown words may be looked up. The children may take notes from your outline on the board. I draw a box around just a few words—the most important ones—for the younger children to copy. Here is an example of an outline of Ephesians 6:11-18 regarding the whole armour of God.

I. Why put it on?
   A To stand against the sneaky tricks of the enemy
   B. We wrestle not against flesh and blood, but . . .
      1. Against principalities
      2. Against powers
      3. Against the rulers of the darkness
      4. Against spiritual wickednes
II. What do we put on?
   A. Truth
   B. Righteousness
   C. Preparation of gospel
   D. Faith
      1. Shield
      2. Most important
      3. Quenches all fiery darts
   E. Salvation
   F. Word of God
III. What else do we do?
   A. Pray
   B. Watch

By outlining the Bible, your students will learn to dig for the hidden treasures in God's word. A selection has to be looked at very carefully before it can be outlined. Let your children study the passage and tell you what to put down next. You can study this way as you read through the Bible. (Luther recommended a New Testament focus.) As you do your daily reading, choose verses to memorize. Drill on these daily. (See "How to Memorize" in Chapter 5, "Combinations")

You could use a Bible curriculum such as *Bible Study Guide for All Ages.* This course includes drills on The Ten Commandments and other important portions of God's word. Hands-on activities are also included. I especially like the daily confession that the children made— "God is telling me to . . ." But you can do this as you read, without a guide or book. Make your own charts, lists, time lines and other aids for learning apostles, books and Commandments. On one chart we made, the good kings were listed on one side and the bad on the other.

Don't let these suggestions keep you from the Word. If you take the time to discuss as you read, and look up words occasionally, both you and children will grow in the Lord with reading alone—especially when this sowing is watered by prayer.

The Family Altar
Home and Health, © 1907, Pacific Press Publishing

The corner-stones of the family altar are love, order, mutual confidence and personal responsibility. How many family altars are broken and falling down for lack of these strong corners! Love for God, for each other—and for prayer—are strangely missing. The children are allowed to whisper, play, sit on the floor, lie on the couch or loll about as they please. The older ones come before God in this sacred gathering-place in any kind of slouchy, dirty dress with a restless air of nervous haste. Little faith or confidence in God are manifested. Father and Mother each doubt the piety of both and because of this strained feeling, and a desire to be through with worship as soon as possible, the father takes

*upon himself all the burden of the family devotion by read-
ing a "short psalm" and "making" a prayer. Is it strange that
children reared in such an atmosphere learn to treat religion
lightly from seeing daily this rude interpretation of it?*

*But conducted as it should be, the family altar is a mighty
factory in the making of a home—a spiritual table where the
bread of life is daily eaten, without haste and where all the
members grow in strength, nearer to God and nearer to each
other. This is the one place of all others where the family circle
is complete. Here the members can look into each other's faces,
speak tender words of comfort and encouragement, sing the
good old songs and read together the words of God. Here
hearts touch each other, and beat in unison and love. When
family ties are woven closer and closer with a binding
strength like this, such cords will hold in the far-off years,
even though the members may be scattered in many lands.*

Prayer

*Around the family altar the children get their first impres-
sions of the importance of prayer and the value and genu-
ineness of the religion of Jesus Christ. How much then, is involved in the faithfulness, promptness and regularity of parents in the observance of this daily privilege! If the hour of
prayer is hurried through with unseemly haste or lightly set
aside for pressing secular duties, the children's estimate of
prayer and religion will be formed accordingly.*

*If worship is held morning and evening at a regular time,
the children will soon learn to expect it. They should be taught
to be in their places at the proper time, with clean hands and
faces, without being "rounded up" and admonished twice
every day. The secret of success in this effort rests in beginning to teach the child the right way when he is very young,
so that he may never know that any other way is ever admis-
sible. Each child, particularly when young, should have his
own proper place and chair, except as rearrangements may*

be made from time to time in tender recognition of the children's wishes. This is not the time for children to be held on anybody's knee, nor should they be allowed to bunch together on the couch or elsewhere. There is too much temptation to play and lounge about under such arrangements. Playthings should be put away. All should give attention, with hands and feet in the proper place, while showing perfect ease and comfort and joy, yet each should recognize that order and respect are due to sacred things.

Hearts United

This is the time to throw off all stiffness and cold restraint; or rather, it is not the proper time and place to put them on. All hearts should blend in perfect love and confidence, which cast out fear. Special temptations may be mentioned, verses from the Bible may be read to meet these temptations or a song may be sung that will give the help needed by some tried or tempted one. Talk freely with the children and help them to see that the family altar is a place for finding comfort, help and forgiveness of sins, as well as joy and freedom from their little cares and troubles. To do this, the nicest tact and wisdom are needed.

Singing

Pass around the song books and the Bibles—or teach your children to come to family altar with their own Bibles. Help the younger ones find their places. Teach all to sing and be sure that they do the best they can. As soon as they are able to read, let them join in the reading around. Those who cannot read will soon learn to follow the others, and thus their attention will be secured and they will feel that they are taking part in the worship, as indeed they are.

The children may be taught to pray at the family altar— and find it a privilege and joy—long before they have been really converted to God. Prayer is much easier if learned from the youngest age, at the time in life when the ABCs of everything are being learned. Frequently at morning worship, it may be proper for only one adult to pray aloud. Such prayers may be closed with the Lord's prayer, in which all can join. The one praying may introduce it with some such fitting words as these, "Let Thy blessing rest upon us all while we join in praying as Thou hast taught us, 'Our Father who art in heaven . . . .' "

In the evening, when there is more time, all the members of the family should have an opportunity to pray. The children who are too young to express their wants independently in prayer, should be encouraged to repeat the little prayer they have been taught to say at their bedsides. Little by little they will be able to add to these in a natural way by praying for some new friend or to be kept from the temptation into which they are most liable to fall. Parents who have never tried this method will be surprised and delighted to find how the children enjoy it and develop the ability to construct their own prayers intelligently. By thus hearing their own voices in public prayer, fear is soon cast away, and they will grow in the knowledge and gifts of prayer as the years go by.

Sterling Character

Even babies can learn character. Every cry, every whim, does not need to be pacified. Character can be built as the infant learns to be at peace within himself. Pray for them during this time. Our children were taught that when they were put to bed, it was bedtime. They soon learned to go to sleep without delay.

Avoid Favorites

Your favorite will be the most difficult to train—and without later diligence and godly intervention—will have the least desirable character. Why? Whether you admit it or not, you are easier on him. His soft life will not be conducive to mighty character. We read about these types in Victorian novels. These mamma's boys (and sometimes girls)—petted and spoiled when young—become incorrigible as young adults. Take some time to consider the personality and mannerisms of your favorite.

✐ Although we do not vocalize our favorite, our attitudes and actions show him or her clearly to all. Favoritism not only weakens the character of the favorite, it can hurt and create bitterness in our other children. If at all present, let it be in heart alone, lifting that one especially to the Lord. It could be that he or she needs special prayer for some future task or challenge.

Be the Example

The very most important part of training character in our children is training our own stubborn wills. We must be "perfect" if we want them to be perfect. We must live the crucified life, with a crucified will. I know this is a tough bite to chew, but so very important. Don't delay. Please don't delay putting your life under the Lordship of Jesus Christ and his Word. Be a doer of the Word. Those children will not delay in growing into the image of what you are! But there is always hope! The Word of God and the Power of God can change and renew even adults, so it can certainly change older children. Live an exemplary life-style of character by always doing the godly thing—by being a faithful doer of the Word.

Admit that you, too, struggle to do right. Let your children know that they are not alone in resisting sin. But don't leave them there. Remind them that both they and you can do all things through Christ, and that His mercies are new every morning—there is always a fresh beginning! Be the one to attack a fault first. Be consistent in your chores and responsibilities and allow nothing less from them.

Strengths and Faults

Focus on your child's strengths. Acknowledge them to your child—and sometimes to others in your child's presence. Notice and mention growth in character or habits (see below for more on habits). This will do more good toward establishing sterling character than the brute force of discipline, for it encourages inward controls in your children.

Help chip away at weaknesses in character by remembering to pray for your children. Assign fitting Bible verses for copywork and memory-work. *Nave's Topical Bible* can be used for this. Be available for counsel. Lastly—especially when beginning to train—there will need to be correction and chastisement.

Read Good Books

After our children began reading independently, we spent most of our read-aloud time with character-building books such as biographies of great people who gave their whole lives to God's work, or books magnifying the beauty of good character traits and the ugliness of bad character. Some fiction models strong and godly character, while other books model the opposite but can also be tools for discussion with your children. "Did the character know God?" "Did he know God's Word?" "Do you like this character?" "Was that a godly thing to do?" "Would that please God?"

Form Habits

Habits are the framework of character. No good habits—no right character. Habits are best initiated early, trained with diligence and maintained with attention. If your children are older, start there! Start with one thing at a time. When that one thing is a habit go on to the next needful area. Do not be content too long with one good habit when others are needing attention. Forming habits produces self-discipline. If we consistently train our flesh to do the hard thing, before long we will have formed good habits, which will result in blessing, peace and ease.

Listing and Doing

❧ Start by making a list of all the good habits you would like to see in your own life. (We can't expect to be successful at training our children if we are untrained ourselves.) Put in as much detail as necessary. Now pick just one of those listed, and put the list away. Do this one thing over and over and over (and over and over and over and over!) until it is a sure habit. Then you will be able to effectively train your children to form their own good habits.

Next make lists for your children as a group or individually. Pick one habit from each child's list to work on. You will have to put the same effort—or more—into this undertaking. Romans 12:8 tells us to rule with diligence. Diligence and self-control are the opposites of laziness and indolence, which cause little or no pain and imply not making the effort to do the right thing consistently. "Diligence," rather, is *marked by persevering and painstaking effort.* These two words hold the key to victory as we commit to forming good habits.

"Painstaking" means *marked by or requiring great pains; very careful and diligent.* The greatest pains are when one begins to form a good habit and break a bad one. It requires great diligence to persevere. "Persevere" means *to persist in or to remain constant to a purpose, an idea, or a task in the face of obstacles or discouragement.* The enemy will put up many obstacles! For instance, if you have never made it a habit to rise at a set time, you will find it much easier to stay in bed. You may be given thoughts such as, "Just one more day won't hurt." But one more day without discipline means that you are many more days from having formed a good habit. I have heard it said that it takes ten days to form habits. *Only ten days!* If we take pains to persevere for ten days, we will be well on our way to success.

Another roadblock the devil puts up is telling us that our efforts are not doing any good, thereby discouraging us—tempting us to discontinue. The enemy does not want us to form good habits. Let's not forget Ephesians 6:12: *For we wrestle not against flesh and blood, but against principalities, against powers, against the rulers of the darkness of this world, against spiritual wickedness in high places.*

We are to be fixed and unchanging—sticking like glue to doing the right thing. The Lord has promised to help us. *He giveth power to the faint; and to them that have no might he increaseth strength* (Is. 40:29). When we step out in obedience, He steps in and empowers us. *For thou hast girded me with strength unto the battle: thou hast subdued under me those that rose up against me. Thou hast also given me the necks of mine enemies; that I might destroy them that hate me. They cried, but there was none to save them: even unto the LORD, but he answered them not. Then did I beat them small as the dust before the wind: I did cast them out as the dirt in the streets* (Ps.18:39-42).

Follow these steps for good habits.

1) First of all, pray. *Watch and pray, that ye enter not into temptation: the spirit indeed is willing, but the flesh is weak* (Matt. 26:41). Be sure to pray that your life will manifest more love. Isn't the failure to form and teach these good habits largely because of selfishness?
2) Make separate detailed lists of needed habits for yourself and for your children, as a group or individually.
3) Form one good habit in your own life, selecting from your list.
4) Train your children in one good habit. Take plenty of time for this. Make it a sure habit before going on to anything else.
5) Praise God for what has been accomplished and go on with one habit at a time. You. Then your children. Until all that needs to be changed is changed habit-wise.
6) Be cautious not to let a habit slip into a non-habit.

Above All is Charity

And let us consider one another to provoke unto love and to good works . . . (Heb. 10:24). *And above all these things put on charity, which is the bond of perfectness* (Col. 3:14).

Since love has such importance in God's eyes, let's make sure we model and teach it. To teach servanthood, be a servant to your children and your spouse, and then to others. Just because you have made the decision to homeschool doesn't mean that you automatically have a loving home. The devil will just work harder to discredit your home. There can easily be a *spirit* of selfishness no matter what you are doing. As a parent, you have the opportunity to provoke your children to love and good works. This is the opposite of provoking to wrath. Provoke means:

- *To create anew, especially by means of the imagination.* This is what the Bible or good literature does.
- *To call to mind by naming, citing, or suggesting.* Remind your children of the joy of loving at Christmas and at other times when they thought of others more than self.
- *To lead or move, as to a course of action, by influence.* Be the example in loving others more than self, within the family and without.
- *To bring about or stimulate the occurrence of; cause.* To persuade or enforce.

Growth is Gradual

Don't be discouraged if you don't see growth, change or a Christian worldview immediately in your children. Mark 4:26-28 says that a *man should cast seed into the ground and should sleep, and rise night and day and the seed should spring and grow up, he knoweth not how. For the earth bringeth forth fruit of herself; first the blade, then the ear, after that the full corn in the ear.*

Loving and teaching (casting seed) is our job while growth in our children is a supernatural work that is automatic and gradual. *For precept must be upon precept, precept upon precept; line upon line, line* upon line; here a little, and there a little (Is. 28:10). Just keep on praying in faith—believing God's promises without wavering. Keep on doing the right things. *Be not weary in well doing: for in due season we shall reap, if we faint not* (Gal. 6:9). In their book, *The Successful Homeschool Family Handbook,* Dr. Raymond and Dorothy Moore provide a Christian values test for older children. Many Christian parents wonder if their children really do agree with Biblical values. We were pleased to find that our children—as most from Christian homes do—passed the test.

Keep on doing the right thing!

There is a very high price to pay if we fail to train our children. *Because thou hast forgotten the God of thy salvation, and hast not been mindful of the rock of thy strength, therefore shalt thou plant pleasant plants, and shalt set it with strange slips: In the day shalt thou make thy plant to grow, and in the morning shalt thou make thy seed to flourish: but the harvest shall be a heap in the day of grief and of desperate sorrow* (Is. 17: 10,11).

However, there is a mighty blessing when we do train our children for God! *I will contend with him that contendeth with thee, and I will save thy children* (Is. 49:25). *And all thy children shall be taught of the LORD; and great shall be the peace of thy children* (Is. 54:13). *As for me, this is my covenant with them, saith the LORD; My spirit that is upon thee, and my words which I have put in thy mouth, shall not depart out of thy mouth, nor out of the mouth of thy seed, nor out of the mouth of thy seed's seed, saith the LORD, from henceforth and for ever* (Is. 59:21).

As God's own, we are a wondrously blessed people. His love for us is unfathomable! He *daily loadeth us with benefits* (Ps. 68:19). *By knowledge shall the chambers be filled with all precious and pleasant riches* (Prov. 24:4). He has given us a sacred trust and gift in our children, so let's be faithful to train them well, in gratitude for that gift—continually sowing the good seeds that will grow into the good harvest of righteousness. ☆*Parenting is our most important mission!*

See "Pursuing Better Parenting" in ❀ *Easy Homeschooling Companion* for more on Biblical parenting systems.

9

Studying Science, Art & Math

Last year the girls made tremendous progress—two to three grade levels ahead in . . . math. —September 6, 1993

The creative and yet easy methods in this chapter prove that learning really can be fun—and not just for the student! You will learn things you never knew, find novel ways to teach math and even learn to draw!

Science

Dr. Arthur Robinson, Charlotte Mason and I agree! Science can be learned from books! Not only can you read biographies and autobiographies of famous scientists, you can read literary scientific books. The best are clear and crisp with an underlying enthusiasm for the topic. (See "How to Choose Literature," Chapter 3. For Dr. Robinson's and Charlotte Mason's views on science teaching, see Chapter 11.)

Choose one area of science to study each year, such as chemistry, physics, meteorology or biology; or study the science of a period along with its history—according to your scope and sequence. Then go on to read biographies of a scientist who worked in the field you have chosen. Be sure to get the oldest biography possible. Some of the newer books are very poorly written and extremely boring!

You will learn scientific facts from biographies—but to learn more, you can expand your study by checking out scientific books on that topic from the children's or adult's department of your public library. If there is objectionable material—such as evolution—you can leave that book there, or skip over that part when reading aloud. My children have learned "creation science" from the Bible and know that there is a wonderful personal God who created them in His image!

Finally, you can attempt an experiment in the field that you have read about. The best experiment books have topically divided chapters, so that as you study a scientist you can easily find an appropriate experiment to do. Suggested experiments should have a one-hundred percent success rate and use extremely common materials—those that you are almost sure to have in your home. Several years ago, my husband brought home a library discard that fit those guidelines. It was George Barr's *More Research Ideas for Young Scientist* from the "Young Scientist" series.

The best formal course we used was from ☞ Bob Jones University. It included a small, simple-to-use, homeschool teacher's manual (not to be confused with a "Teacher's Manual," which is to be avoided at all costs, no matter what the subject!).

We learned about rocket science at a science museum in a bordering state. Another time we explored strobe-light science and other concepts at a nearby museum. More than a day is needed to thoroughly study the topics presented at science museums, so if you have ready access, visit often.

The Scientific Method

✔ You can use the Scientific Method for your experiments, research and nature studies (See Chapter 6). It encompasses:
  • Observation. Look carefully at the specimen being studied.
  • Interpretation. What is happening?
  • Classification. Identify. Find Latin name.
  • Recording. Sketch and make journal entries.
  • Discovering. Research and study to learn even more.
  • Prediction. What will happen next or in a similar situation?

Science is LOOKing at what God made!

Art

In third grade, art class consisted of completing the teacher's cookie-cutter projects. My college instructor's idea of art was globs of paint "thrown" on a canvas. Then I attended Ringling School of Art in Sarasota, Florida where I was introduced to real art training. This was a serious art school. We even drew from live naked models. (I am mentioning this in case you have older students considering this route.) We also had individual classes in color and design, perspective, and still life. The school offered majors in commercial art, fine arts and fashion design.

I also attended Traphagen School of Fashion in New York and fulfilled a childhood dream of learning design and patternmaking. In Hawaii, I did free-lance fashion art for local businesses and worked as an assistant designer. I have done pen and ink drawings, portraits and oil paintings.

✍ With all my art training, I had neglected practice over the years. When I decided to illustrate this book, I found myself with deadlines and other tasks to attend to. Thus the sketches herein were done quickly. Some I like more than others, but all could be done more professionally. I had wanted illustrations in the first edition, so *am* thankful that it is finally a reality.

In teaching art to my own children, I was totally inexperienced. Our homeschool's focus was literary, rather than the fine and applied arts. Nevertheless, our children have not had to wait twenty years to get good art training. We began with ☞ *Drawing with Children* and our children learned the same basic principles I learned when much older. Of course with the motor skills that they had at two to six years of age, the results were not quite as good. They did well enough, though, to win purple and blue ribbons at our county fair!

Learning to Draw

Learning to draw well is the essence of art training. Although Picasso is remembered for his abstract "cubism," even *he* was trained to draw well and did some absolutely lovely life-like drawings and paintings.

You and your children can learn together in all subjects. Art is no exception. Although art materials traditionally are expensive, you can use copy paper, regular pencils and Crayola® markers from Wal-Mart.

Art class may take more time than other classes, but after you have finished your own work of art, you can read aloud to your children while they are finishing theirs.

An Artist's Eye

The first step in drawing is learning to really see things as they are—developing an artist's "eye." Draw most often from real objects, real people, scenery—sometimes from photographs or other good and simple artwork—but not from memory. Another good reason for drawing from life is to get the proper shading and highlights which are almost impossible to apply correctly otherwise.

Look carefully at your subject, noting such things such as proportion and shape. In art—maybe even more than in other subjects—practice makes perfect! The more you and your children sketch—following these guidelines—the better artists you will be.

What to Look For

Look for the shapes in your subject. Before you put a pencil to the paper, discuss and spend time identifying and discussing the shapes in the scene or still life, and shapes within shapes. Do you see an oval? Perhaps the sky is a big rectangle, behind the circle of leaves and long rectangle of the tree trunk. Some of these won't be so obvious—such as the perfect circle that encloses the upper bodies (arms, head, veil, etc.) in Picasso's *The Lovers*. Practice drawing only the shapes you see, emphasizing their geometry. Monet said it this way:

> *When you go out to paint, try to forget what objects you have before you—a tree, a field, or whatever. Merely think, "Here is a little square of blue, here is an oblong of pink, here a streak of yellow." And paint it just as it looks to you—the exact color and shape . . . .*[1]

Always look for proportions. Check by holding a pencil at arm's length. When sketching a person standing, for instance, check this way. The point of the pencil will be at the top of the head and your thumbnail should be placed on the pencil at the chin line. Holding your thumbnail in position, see how many heads tall the figure is. Then transfer that proportion to your paper. You can do this in checking the proportion of other details too.

A Light Touch

When sketching, always use a light touch. Only darken and add shading when you are sure your composition is the way you want it. When your whole composition is laid down in proper proportions, add deep and dramatic shading, or less shading and more outlining.

Lesson Ideas

1) Practice observing, and then draw only the outlines of the items in your subject.
2) Practice shading evenly. I found that even my best artists needed this practice.
3) On another day, take particular note of the shadows and highlights and put them in—in excess and without outlines. Many of the "masters" emphasized shading and highlighting, which resulted in dramatic and interesting paintings. (See Rembrandt's paintings when doing this lesson.)

Media Choices

When your students are proficient at seeing and sketching, you can go on to different media (materials). ☞ Berol Prismacolor® pencils are soft and blend well—if time is taken to shade gradually. We kept them usable for many years by keeping them exclusively for our special art projects. You will need a small inexpensive art pencil sharpener because most sharpeners cut off too much wood and pigment.

Charcoal can be messy. Pastels are colorful and blend easily—but also smear easily. I used ☞ Kohinoor Rapidograph® pens in art school but there are now less expensive disposable pens that give equally good results. *Drawing with Children* suggests colored markers. I purchased Crayola® markers but, if at all possible, use art store markers because the discount store markers run and keep your little ones' gorgeous works from being all they could be. They did not prevent our children's works from getting blue and purple ribbons, though!

Mixing Colors

✔ Here's a project for colored pencils or paint (you may use inexpensive watercolor box paints). Observe and match the colors in a subject. Practice with just the primary colors (red, yellow, blue). You will soon know almost instinctively that your grayed blue needs a tiny bit more red to match the violet shadows. Mix your colors on a plastic palette or a Styrofoam® meat tray. When you start easel or on-site painting, you can cut a thumb hole in the meat tray.

Watercolors

The best and easiest watercolor technique I've seen is "Fast and Loose" developed by Ron Ranson.[2]

Mr. Ranson uses few colors, few details, few brushes and very few strokes to produce lovely scenic paintings. You can lean your watercolor pad against a tree, so an easel is not absolutely necessary. My husband built easels for the children one Christmas and painted them in bright primary colors.

How to Paint Scenery

- Go to the scene. Select a good view for your composition. Search out a single dominant feature, but don't put it right in the middle of your paper.
- Using your hake brush (see art supplies below), quickly lay a thin layer of a very pale gray across your sky.
- Rinse your brush (always rinse between colors and change your water often) and mix a blue wash—not too intense, but more intense than the first wash.
- Now again, quickly lay some sky in, leaving white places for clouds—bigger shapes toward the top of your paper and smaller near the horizon (bottom of your sky). Remember, stay quick and loose. Clouds are not distinct ovals, but puffs of imbalanced smoke.
- Now with a gray put in a bit of shading at the bottoms of your clouds. *Isn't that beautiful?!*
- Now put in distant trees in a soft grayed color, again with your hake brush held at an angle and daubed on.
- Stroke on nearby tree roots and bottoms of trunks with the one-inch flat brush or the hake held perpendicularly to the paper. The nearby leaves are daubed on with the hake brush held at an angle.
- Next, the few darker branches that show through the leaves are flipped on with the rigger brush. Lift the tip off quickly making the end of the branch thinner than its base.
- Use a quick flip of your fingernail to cut highlights along these branches (and into rivers and streams as well).
- Waterways are also done "fast and loose." One or two strokes with the flow is all you need. Where different colors of wet paint meets wet, leave a tiny white area to avoid running, but if you do have some running, don't worry about it. That's part of the charm of watercolor painting!
- Put one other darker shading color at the bottom of the trees.
- Make short reflections in the water. Add whatever other shading or small amount of indistinct detail your painting needs, and you are done! Beautiful and easy.

Look for books and videos on Mr. Ranson's method at bookstores, Hobby Lobby or **www.amazon.com**, but check your library first—that's where we got the video *Fast & Loose*.

A similar method can be used with oils paints or acrylics, although these types of paints are worked much more. Because oils dry very slowly and colors usually become muddy if mixed while wet on the canvas, they are better for the studio. There you can work on the painting in stages, letting each step dry over a period of days. Oil is easier to work with than acrylic, in my opinion. I like the blending option and the richer, old-world appearance of the pigments.

Acrylic, although a quick-drying medium, has a somewhat plasticized (exactly what it is) appearance, and colors do not seem to blend as well. Experiment. Get the primary colors and white. (White is not necessary with water colors; just leave the paper blank.) Mix your colors and attempt to paint some simple sketches.

My favorite media—pen, ink & oils.

Art Supplies

These are listed in order of importance. Most are available from Hobby Lobby or other art supply stores.

1) *Pencils.* Drawing pencils are graded from B (soft) and H (hard). I prefer a softer pencil with a light touch for initial sketching, then heavier pressure for shading. Choose a harder (lighter) pencil for rough sketching for children who tend to have a naturally heavy hand.

2) *Paper.* Any paper is okay for pencil, but you may wish to purchase a supermarket drawing pad for markers, and watercolor paper for paints. (Ron Ranson suggests 140 pound, 12" x 16" or 16" x 20" sheets for easel painting.)

3) *A kneaded eraser.* Comes in a small block, but should be pulled apart and pushed together (kneaded) often. This eraser is best because does not damage paper.

4) *Berol Prismacolor pencils.* Available separately or in sets at art supply stores. To save money, instead of a complete set get the primary colors, or greens and browns and blues for nature drawings.

5) *Watercolors.* Mr. Ranson recommends seven colors—raw sienna, ultramarine, lemon yellow, Payne's gray, burnt umber, alazarin crimson and light red.

6) *Brushes.* Mr. Ranson recommends:
   - A two-inch Japanese "Hake" brush.
   - A #3 long haired "rigger."
   - A one-inch flat nylon or man-made brush. This brush is only used for sharp edges, such as buildings and fences.

If these brushes are out of your price range, look—as I did—for similar less expensive brushes. With acrylic and oil paints, you may need other brushes.

7) *Pigments, etc.* Oils (easier to blend), acrylics (faster drying), pastels, drawing pens, ink, and so on.

8) ☞ ***Art teaching books.*** All the books listed in Resources teach how to draw well, but you may not need a book if you follow the above instructions and spend a lot of time just drawing. Check your library for art books, history and technique videos, and biographies of artists; search the Internet for drawing tutorials.

Art History

Study history with the art of that period and culture. Pick up big, beautiful art books at your library or borrow ☞ **National Gallery of Art** videos, such as "Old Masters" (Blake, Rembrandt, Goya, etc.), "Modern Masters" (Monet, Cezanne, Renoir, Picasso, Gauguin), and "American Art" (Copley, Cassatt, and some primitive artists). As do most art galleries and art schools, these videos display the unclothed body in some of the works. "American Art" is one exception. Preview the tape, so that you know exactly where to stop and fast forward.

Math Writing

Although I enjoyed learning math, I had little interest in teaching it. Then I discovered "Math Writing" which combines reading, writing and math. *Perfect!* Students make up stories about individual numbers, read children's books about numbers and learn math concepts by thought, discussion, writing and drawing. Students keep math journals and teachers keep portfolios of the students' math writing. Math writing is a stress-free, easy method!

Marilyn Burns originated math writing in 1975 with *The I Hate Mathematics! Book.* Past issues of *Instructor* magazine gave me much information.³ Marilyn says:

> *Writing in math class has two major benefits. It supports students' learning because, in order to get their ideas on paper, children must organize, clarify and reflect on their thinking . . . also benefits teachers . . . writing is a window into what they [the students] understand, how they approach ideas, what misconceptions they harbor and how they feel about what they're discovering.*

When you begin using these methods, Marilyn suggests talking with your students about these reasons for math writing—focusing on the fact that they will be helping *you* by writing in math class. Later, discussion before each session helps the words flow more easily when the child begins to write independently.

"Divide thirteen eggs into four equal parts?"

Technique

Start with one problem such as dividing 13 eggs, 13 candy bars and $13.00 among 4 people. Or have your students examine and write about the difference between two fractions, such as 1/2 and 1/3. After discussion "write a prompt on the board for children to use if they wish. For example: 'I think the answer is_____. I think this because_____.'" This should get them started. Then have them revise and edit so that their writing clearly shows they understand. Encourage them to add detail, telling exactly how they came to their conclusions. Post a list of the different mathematical words you are studying so that it can be referred to when your child is writing. Spelling and grammar can be corrected and a final draft done. Illustrations may be added. Finally, have them read their papers aloud.

To use calculators, have them first do the problem the traditional way and then check with the calculator. Other times your student could first use a calculator and then explain—write and read their papers aloud, telling how they arrived at each solution. "They may write about any idea . . . as long as it makes sense to them and they can explain it." Marilyn says that if the children can explain the process they used to arrive at the answer, they are learning, whether they used a calculator or their brains.

Math Journals

Have your children keep math journals. Tell your students to "include something you learned, you're not sure about or you're wondering about." Marilyn Burns also suggests keeping a portfolio of each child's work. Let the child choose which papers to keep. Have them write about why they chose that particular paper and what they learned in that lesson. Add to their choices your selections—focusing on those that show your child's mathematical thinking skills.

Picture Books

Another literary concept is to check out a picture book from the library that has a number theme and use that as the basis for a math lesson. For example, with a counting book about animals, the lesson could be about finding out how many of each type or color, then how many animals in all, and so forth. Use manipulatives—even for older children—and let the children use their creativity and individuality. Games can also play a part in this system of math teaching. After the activity, go on and have your children do their math writing about the topic that you have just discussed, book you have just read, game you have just played, problem or solution that your child has just discovered or created.

Here's a passage from the Bible that you could use for your math lesson with questions following:

So all the generations from Abraham to David are fourteen generations; and from David until the carrying away into Babylon are fourteen generations; and from the carrying away into Babylon unto Christ are fourteen generations (Matt. 1:17).

Ask your child: "Does God divide things equally?" "How many generations from Abraham to Christ?" "Think of alternate ways to compute these generations." "How many years is a generation?" "How many generations from Christ to _____?" And so on. (Your students may have to do research.) After discussion, your child can go on and do math writing.

Philosophy

Marilyn Burns says that we should let the children push the curriculum and not vise-versa. She offers some good advice when she says to focus on depth rather than covering many things lightly. This should be a priority in other subjects as well. Don't allow yourself to be pushed. More real progress will be made if fewer concepts are covered more deeply. And don't eliminate drill! The basic math facts need to be drilled until they are second nature.

Scope & Sequence

To use math writing exclusively as a replacement for workbooks or textbooks, use a guide such as ☞ **Typical Course of Study** to find out which concepts are covered at your child's age. Just don't think you have to do everything in the guide! Your elementary age child has quite a few years to learn, and learn well, the math basics of adding, subtracting, multiplying, dividing, time, money, fractions, story-problems and decimals. Many things are taught that need not be, as they are naturally assimilated by the child over the years. Math writing makes your child comfortable with math concepts and lays a good foundation for mathematical thinking.

You can also use a workbook or textbook. We have used *Saxon* texts with good results. No matter what method or materials you use for math, Marilyn reminds us that partial learning is natural to the learning process. So let's delight in experiencing this process, and not become impatient for the end result!

How we will apply what we learn and why we need it should also be taught. The highest goal for all learning is to please God and be trained for his service and glory.

10
Gleaning from History

A child's education should begin at least one hundred years before he was born.[1]

In this chapter we will examine the history of education to glean ideas for schooling our children today. I have searched my library of old books[2] and distilled the pedagogy of the past. I have also looked to the Word of God for the teaching methods of Jesus Christ.

The Hebrews

The education of the earliest Hebrews centered around the family. The notion of the state is almost unknown—God is the real king, while the perfect man is pious and virtuous, capable of attaining the ideal traced by God himself in these terms—*Ye shall be holy: for I the Lord your God am holy* (Lev. 19:2).

The child, then, was to become the faithful servant of Jehovah. To this end it was not needful that he should be learned, but only that he should know God's laws and ordinances. These were first taught by the oral communication and instructive example of the parents. Fathers also taught their children the nation's history and the great events that had marked the destiny of the people of God.

✐ The discipline given to children was unwavering in firmness, proven by many passages in the Bible. Some say it was too harsh, and yet children grew in character and were kept from evil in learning *the fear of the Lord*. It was Almighty God who was to be pleased, not "almighty child." Today we are too quick to avoid offending the child, and the modern-day, child-rights advocates, while God and his *perfect parenting patterns* are often being given second place. *For the wisdom of this world is foolishness with God . . .* (1 Cor. 3:19).

At the time of Christ, Jewish boys entered school at the age of six. They were taught reading, writing, a little of natural history and a great deal of geometry and astronomy. Naturally, the Bible was the first book put in their hands. The master interspersed moral lessons with the teaching of reading and made a special effort to secure a correct pronunciation. He multiplied his explanations in order to make sure of being understood, repeating his comments even to the four-hundredth time if necessary. It seems that the methods were suggestive and attractive and—at this time—the discipline relatively mild.

We are told by Renan in his *Vie de Jésus* that "Jesus doubtless learned to read and write according to the method of the East, which consists in putting into the hands of the child a book which he repeats in concert with his comrades till he knows it by heart."

God provides the perfect parenting pattern.

The Greeks

Some consider Greek culture the epitome of learning, knowledge, art, wisdom and democracy. Yet, in the Greek republics, the individual was always subordinate to the State. With the Greeks, the State appears distinctly and avowedly as the educator.

Sparta

At Sparta, training for military strength was foremost. Virtues and good manners were insisted upon, while clear-cut and incisive judgments were systematically cultivated. Spartans were taught to suffer without showing it. They were taught self control and to be honest—yet they were trained to slyly steal upon occasions. They were frequently asked to critique particular citizens—with the guidelines that their comments be short and to the point—and to include supporting arguments. They learned by listening to discussions, about state affairs, by mature and experienced men.

Athens

In Athens, the training of the mind prevailed. At the age of seven, a teacher—usually a slave—was charged with the oversight of the child. The pupil attended schools from sunrise to sunset and studied grammar, physical education and music. Arithmetic was elementary. Later, drawing, geometry and geography were added to the curriculum.

The students were taught to sing and play stringed instruments to fulfill their patriotic and religious duties. "Music," Aristotle said, "brings harmony." For reading, they first learned letters and then spelled easy syllables and words. When sufficiently skilled in this, the teacher dictated to them portions of poems. Homer was used to teach history, reading and mythology. Sometimes lessons were given in the open air.

Socrates

Socrates taught by questioning that compelled his students to form clear ideas. His purpose was to convince men of their errors and in so doing to confound their arrogance. He also hoped, by this questioning, to teach truth. (The Sophists, rather, taught that victory in argument was more important than truth.) Two types of questions were used by Socrates:

1) *Ironical questions convinced of error.* A man was led on step by step until suddenly and unexpectedly, he was brought face to face with the logical consequences of his opinion; thus either convinced of his error, or rendered unable to maintain it with argument.

2) *Maieutic or birth-giving questions developed a fundamental truth.* Men whose opinions or purposes in life were not yet clearly formed were questioned as in ironical questioning.

✔ Here's how to use the Socratic Method with your children. Keep in mind cause and effect (consequences of actions or beliefs). Then, start with their position if they have one, or with a position of society. Make sure the initial questions are closely aligned with the original position. Slowly lead by a series of questions to the logical conclusion. Use of this method will help your children become independent thinkers.

According to Plato, "moral power" resulted from bodily exercise and a continual feasting on the good and beautiful—including carefully selected religious books. (Although he believed that God should be honored by lives of justice and virtue, Plato also believed that the child belonged to the state and that only the fit had the right to live.)

Aristotle was the "greatest of all the Greek philosophers, a man of a genuinely scientific mind" and a master of induction (deriving general principles from particular facts or instances). He countered Plato's communism with teachings that family love was the foundation of social life but did not go so far as to relinquish the teaching of the children to the family.

The Romans

Rome's tremendous power resulted from the home life that prevailed until wealth and luxury began their corrupting influences. There was a freedom and dignity vested in Roman motherhood unique in the pagan world. This resulted in home influences which were both powerful and ennobling. The charming Roman mother is represented by Cornelia placing her hands on the heads of her boys and speaking of them as her "jewels."

It seems to have been quite common for girls as well as boys to attend elementary schools. The first schools were military and religious. Students recited a "catechism" containing the names of the gods and goddesses, and studied the Twelve Tables (law). The fruit of this education was robust, courageous, disciplined and very patriotic citizens. The virtues of Rome were the result of:

- Firm family discipline, with strong paternal authority
- The high esteem—almost the equal of man—of the mother's position as guardian of the family circle and the teacher of her children
- A regularity and exactness of the most ordinary acts of daily life, which was the result of their religion
- The training from youth to consider the law as natural, inviolable and sacred

Unfortunately, Greek ideas conquered Rome.

Rome then conquered Greece and Greek ideas—including their ideas of education—conquered Rome. The children were then entrusted to a pedagogue, whose faults and vices were overlooked. The slave who was a drunkard or glutton—unfit for any other work—was placed over the children as teacher.

But the Romans never considered education as a duty of the state. "Our ancestors," said Cicero, "did not wish that children should be educated by fixed rules, determined by the laws, publicly promulgated and made uniform for all."

After the age of Augustus, education became more and more an affair of oratory. Quintillion said, "Has a son been born to you? From the first conceive the highest hopes of him." He goes on to say that minds that rebel against all instruction are unnatural—most often it is the training which is at fault, not nature. He also says that a student's language shall be irreproachable, learning Greek even before their native language.

The Trivium

1) Nine- to eleven-year olds should be taught demanding memory work—their strength. "Let study be to him a play; ask him questions; commend him when he does well; and . . . let him enjoy the consciousness of his little gains in wisdom." Writing practice

should contain, "not senseless maxims, but moral truths." Quintillion did not counsel haste in any case. "We can scarcely believe how progress in reading is retarded by attempting to go too fast."

2) As soon as the child could read and write (twelve to fourteen) he was taught grammar and rhetoric. Composition and narratives accompanied the study of the rules of grammar. At this time geometry, music and philosophy were also studied. All of these, according to Quintillion, were instruments for an education in oratory.

3) At fourteen to sixteen, the child was to begin to study philosophy, physics or the science of nature, and morals—all of which furnish the orator with ideas—and logic which teaches him the art of distributing them in a consecutive line of argument. He also learned geometry as a discipline of the mind and music to cultivate a sense of harmony.

Seneca said, "We should learn, not for the sake of school, but for the purposes of life," *non scholœ, sed vitœ discimus*. He also criticized confused and ill-directed reading that does not enrich the understanding and recommended the profound study of a single book, *timeo hominem unius libri*. He said that the best way of being taught is to teach, *docendo discimus,* and that "the end is attained sooner by example than by precept," *longum iter per prœcepta, breve per exempla*.

The history of Rome proves that the best educator is the family, God's government on earth.

The Methods of the Master
Scriptures references are from the book of Matthew, unless otherwise noted.

Jesus Christ's most intimate teaching was reserved for those who would be teaching others. Before beginning, and regularly during His ministry, He prepared spiritually. We too begin by sitting at His feet and receiving His special guidance.

Christ taught everywhere. He modeled the command that was given us specifically as parents to *talk of them when thou sittest in thine house, and when thou walkest by the way, and when thou liest down, and when thou risest up* (Deut. 6:7).

His method was personal dialog, but sometimes—as with large groups—the Master used the "lecture" method. He read aloud (in the temple) and used the Word. *When Jesus had ended these sayings, the people were astonished at his doctrine: for he taught them as one having authority, and not as the scribes* (12:40-42).

When he opened His mouth, truth after truth flowed out in streams of living water. We can also speak with wisdom and authority if we have spent time in God's Word.

He didn't mind being interrupted (9:18,19) and often was, by questions that led to further teaching and discussion (12:38-45). He also, by questioning, stirred His hearers to deep thought (11:7-14). He made sure His listeners understood His teaching (13:51) and the value of their learning (13:53). His teaching was keyed to the comprehension of the listener—in His conversation with the learned Nicodemus, He plunged at once into the most profound doctrines; when He talked with the Samaritan woman, His approach to the truth was most simple and gradual. He didn't hesitate to correct and was stern when necessary but always spoke truth and righteousness. Even in sternness, His motive was love (12:34).

An Activist

Jesus was an activist. He inspired to endure, to expect victory. Like Churchill's "We will not surrender," Christ's words also inspire to victory. Even statements like *ye shall be hated of all men for my name's sake: but he that endureth to the end shall be saved,* set a fire burning within saying, "Yes! I will endure until the end! What honor to be hated for His name's sake!" Jesus modeled for His "students" strong faith in the midst of storms (8:25,26) and was positive and encouraging (9:2; 14:27).

He didn't just *teach* His students, but became involved in their personal lives. He was motivated by compassion and met physical needs immediately and readily (14:14-22). He wanted his hearers whole in body and spirit, as well as mind. He knew that faith came by hearing the Word, and faith was the key to total wellness, so He taught much.

Jesus physically fed His students (14:20) and took time for rest even in the midst of demands (8:18). (We should make sure that we are feeding our children nutritious foods. This can make a major difference in the atmosphere of our homes, and resting as needed will help maintain peace and patience.)

Jesus taught using parables. A parable is a simple story illustrating a moral or religious lesson. A story keeps interest high. A story gets students thinking. A parable reveals more to the spiritually sensitive than to those dull of hearing. Although listeners would not always understand, Jesus would explain eventually—at least to his chosen twelve.

He taught with illustrations from nature. Walking the fields with his disciples, He drew lessons from the plants, the birds, the sowing of the farmer, the gathering of fruit from the vineyard, the ripening harvests and the whispering breezes:

Consider the lilies of the field how they grow; behold the fowls of the air; a sower went forth to sow; lift up your eyes and look on the fields, for they are white and ready to harvest; the wind bloweth where it listeth (Luke 12:24, Matt. 6:26, Matt. 13:3, John 4:35, John 3:8).

The Early Christians

Christianity—by its dogmas, by its concept of the equality of all human creatures, by its spirit of charity—introduced new elements into the conscience and gave a powerful impetus to the moral education of men. Christianity raised the poor and disinherited from their condition of misery and promised them the same instruction. The essence of equal rights for all is contained in the doctrine of Christianity.

They rejected a corrupt and perverse world.

The early Christians came to a common hatred of classical literature and pagan religion. How could they receive with sympathy the literary and scientific inheritance of a society whose morals they hated? The Christian was detached from the commonwealth of man, to enter into the commonwealth of God. He must break with a corrupt and perverse world.

Early Church Fathers

During the first centuries, all education related to the interests of the church. The monasteries were the sole centers of learning until the crusades brought new life to education. Schools and universities were then established. Eventually the Teutonic peoples (Germans, Anglo-Saxons, Scandinavians) began to play a bigger part in education.

The Catechumen schools for adults—and later for children—first taught people about their new faith; they later added reading and writing. Previous to this, instruction was given by tutors or parents in homes, or in pagan schools. Reading, writing, Scripture and Psalms were taught first at Odessa's Christian Common School at the close of the second century.

Clement of Alexandria (150-220)

- Faith is the cornerstone of knowledge.
- Mosaic law and heathen philosophy both prepared the way for Christianity, which is the fulfillment of law and philosophy.
- He sought to harmonize philosophy and religion.

Origen (186-253)

- Never teach pupils anything that you do not yourself practice.
- The end of education is to grow into the likeness of God.
- Pupils must be taught to investigate for themselves.
- The teacher must seek to correct bad habits, as well as give instruction.

Basil the Great (329-379)

Basil urged the use of classic literature. He also said that:
- Punishment should be an exercise in self-command to help to correct the fault—if a child has been quarrelsome, give him solitude and fasting.
- The Bible should be the chief textbook.
- Good habits and right precepts should be taught while children are young.

Chrysostom (347-407)

Educated in pagan schools, Chrysostom, an eloquent educator, kept true to the faith of his devout Christian mother. He believed:
- The teacher should lower himself to the capacity of the pupils in order to elevate them.
- The teacher must not do for the pupils what they can do for themselves.
- Teachers and parents must be the example of Christ. This is the foundation.
- Mothers are the natural educators of children.
- Religious instruction is an essential factor of school work.

The Bible is our chief textbook.

Tertullian (150-230)

In 529, pagan schools were destroyed and education was in the hands of the Church for one thousand years. During those years the ideas of Tertullian and Augustine were foremost. Tertullian was the father of Christian Latin Literature. He opposed anything pagan, and claimed that philosophy made men arrogant and less inclined to faith.

Augustine (354-430)

Augustine's quest for God is detailed in *Confessions*, written in chapters corresponding with the ages of his life. Augustine also condemned classic literature (although indebted to it for his intellectual greatness) and believed it must be excluded from the school. He also believed:
- All teaching is based on faith and authority.
- The chief subject is history pursued in the narrative.
- Abundant use of observation should be used in instruction.
- The teacher must be earnest and enthusiastic.

Middle Ages

Scholasticism, called the philosophy of the Middle Ages, attempted to harmonize ancient philosophy—especially that of Aristotle—with the writings of the church fathers. It covered a period reaching from the ninth to the fifteenth century and was divided into two schools. The master of one was Thomas Aquinas (1225-1274) who exalted the understanding. The other was Duns Scotus (1265-1308) who taught that the will was the highest principle. Faith and knowledge were foundational principles, but the focus changed from literary studies to foolish questions. When knowledge attempted to assume a position above faith, Scholasticism began to self-destruct. Fleury, a seventeenth-century educator, judged Scholasticism when he said, "Philosophizing on words and thoughts . . . was certainly an easy way of getting along without knowledge of the facts . . . which can be acquired only by reading."

Charlemagne

Seven feet tall and commanding in appearance, Charlemagne was a "self-made" man. Trained as a knight, crowned ruler in 800, he then applied himself to Latin, Greek, grammar, rhetoric, logic, music, astronomy and natural history. He established a palace school for his and his courtiers' children. Although he believed in religious training, he insisted that intelligent patriotism should also be given great importance. He took authority over the church and required monks to teach outside of monasteries, introducing compulsory education. Reading, writing, arithmetic and singing were taught.

Alfred the Great

Alfred did not learn to read until he was twelve, yet later gave much attention to literary matters. He became king of the West Saxons in 871 at the age of twenty-three and was very methodical. He divided his day into three equal portions of eight hours each for 1) attending to his work of government, 2) religious devotion and study and 3) sleep, rest and recuperation. He urged that each child be taught Latin, and to read and write.

Knights & Ladies

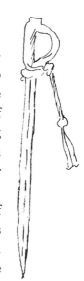

Knights had different ideas of education. Skills, politeness and knightly manners were far more important to them than the ability to read and write. They learned the seven "perfections"—horsemanship, swimming, use of bow and arrow, swordsmanship, hunting, chess-playing and verse-making. The first seven years were spent in the home where obedience, politeness, respect for older persons and religious training prevailed.

At age seven, the knight was put under the care of the lady whom he served as page. Music, poetry, chess and simple intellectual studies were taught at this stage. He also received stricter training under the care of some friendly knight. At fourteen, the boy left the service of his lady and became an esquire to the knight. He then attended his master upon the chase, at tournaments, and in battle. At twenty-one he was knighted, taking vows to speak the truth, defend the weak, honor womanhood and use his sword for the defense of Christianity.

The knight learned godly virtues.

The girls remained at home and were taught domestic arts, etiquette, reading, writing and poetry. In some castles, there were schools for girls where they also learned French, Latin, singing and religion.

The Crusades

The three major crusades occurred between 1096-1192 and drew Christian nations together in one common purpose—to defend and deliver the Holy Land from infidels (unbelievers). Results were 1) increased knowledge of the East, 2) increased commerce and 3) a widened horizon of thought—preparing Europe for intellectual and religious revival. It has been said that the crusades saved Europe and the world from intellectual and spiritual extinction.

The "Church"—whose goal was the teaching of dogmas rather than training the intelligence—had almost entire control of education. The teachers read or recited lectures, the pupils learned by heart. Discipline was harsh.

Universities

Cathedral and monastery schools were forerunners of universities, which began when scholars and students joined themselves together for the purpose of study and investigation. The greatest university of the Middle Ages was that of Paris, which attracted at least twenty thousand students. Its chancellor loved the people with a spirit of sweetness and goodness. He demanded of his teachers patience and tenderness. "Little children," he said, "are more easily managed by caresses than by fear. No living being is more in danger than the child of allowing himself to be corrupted by another child." The child should be protected from "every evil influence, and, in particular, against pernicious literature." In England, Oxford was established in 1140, and Cambridge in 1200.

Love and kindness conquer, hardness destroys.

The Renaissance

The Renaissance encompassed discovery, exploration and inventions. It lessened the hold of the Catholic church over the minds of men, preparing the way for the Reformation. A new appreciation of classical languages resulted in the revival of learning. Printing now made the study of classic works possible.

Men suddenly found intensely human life in the tales of gods and goddesses. These myths became revelations of human expression, strength and beauty. The Renaissance men also noted that these works were written in a polished and charming style. (The *Charlotte Mason Companion,* by Karen Andreola, includes a chapter on Greek myth.)

Petrarch (1304-1374)

Petrarch was the first great leader of the Renaissance. Boccacio, another leader, learned Greek and translated Homer, and also wrote *Decameron,* which inspired and provided material for the first great English poem, *Canterbury Tales,* by Chaucer.

Some of the Renaissance leaders, especially in Italy, introduced not only the beauty of pagan cultures but also their licentiousness. Even Petrarch's writings were interpreted differently by the two groups. One believed there was to be enjoyment without restraint; the other, that achievement and enjoyment were to be for God's glory.

When Constantinople fell into the hands of the Turks in 1453, many Greek scholars fled to Italy carrying their literary treasures with them, expanding the resurgence of learning. However, this learning could not be confined to Italy.

While scholars in Italy focused on learning the classical languages so as to be able to read the classic literature of Greece and Rome, in the Teutonic countries the new knowledge was used to discover the truth and beauty of the New Testament. The study of God's Word wrought changes in many as they accepted its simple truths. Then arose the desire to study Hebrew. Much of this interest can be traced to the Brethren of the Common Life and Thomas á Kempis (author of *Imitatio Christi—Imitation of Christ*) who was a member. The leaders of this order also stressed the teaching of the scriptures in the languages of the people.

Erasmus (1469-1536)

Erasmus was one of the greatest of all Renaissance humanists. His most fruitful work was his edition of the Greek New Testament. He wanted people to study the living Christ as portrayed vividly in the Gospels, so they might find in Him the inspiration for noble living. He said:

> *I long for the day when the husbandman shall sing portions of them [gospels, epistles] to himself as he follows the plough, when the weaver shall hum them to the time of his shuttle, when the traveler shall wile away the weariness of his journey with their stories.*

Regarding education, Erasmus said that lessons should be adapted to the ability of the child and should be taught with sympathy and tenderness. He believed that all subjects should be subordinate to the classics. Geography and other subjects should be taught only for a greater understanding of the classics. He knew that politeness has a moral side, proceeding from the inner disposition of a well-ordered soul.

The duty of instructing the young includes several elements, the first and also the chief of which is that the tender mind of the child should be instructed in piety; the second, that he love and learn the liberal arts; the third, that he be taught tact in the conduct of social life; and the fourth, from his earliest age he accustom himself to good behavior, based on moral principles.

Renaissance learning opened the way for a new intelligence and inspiration for many, struck a sturdy blow for human liberty and began a radical transformation of Christendom.

The Reformation

The invention of printing by Gutenberg in the middle of the fifteenth century was a primary force that brought about universal education—a hallmark of the Reformation. With this tool, Martin Luther (1483-1546) took on the reformation of education, along with the reformation of religion. He is the originator of the first organized schools which were the forerunners of modern schools, with their state support and supervision.

Character begins with learning what is right, and Luther learned right by learning obedience to his parents. He was trained to upright character, hard work and piety, and was given the best education his father could afford. At age fourteen, he had among his teachers some of the Brothers of the Common Life. About a year later, Martin transferred to another school where he soon outstripped his companions in eloquence, languages and poetic verse. Later, at University, he studied grammar, logic and rhetoric—all precision tools of thought and verbal expression—and graduated second in his class, which was no small honor at the second best university in Germany. A few months later with a "storm in his soul," he entered the monastery, leaving his law library behind—taking only Plautus and Virgil. The rest, as they say, is history.

Luther's driving force was to "make the people acquainted with the Word of God." The previous humanistic spirit was almost entirely swallowed up in enthusiasm for Scripture study. A writer hostile to the Reformation wrote, "Even shoemakers, women and ignorant people are eagerly reading the New Testament as the fountain of all truth, with such frequency that they know it by heart." Luther's German version of the New Testament (1524) was based on the Greek text of Erasmus.

The Primary School

The Primary School was the child of Protestantism and its cradle was the Reformation. Luther believed that parents were responsible for their children's education before anyone else, but that the State had a duty to require regular attendance at school. He wrote to magistrates appealing to them to establish and support Christian schools because he felt a Christian responsibility for training all children in godly ways.

But Luther's school was not as structured as what government schools are today. He said that children should attend school only one or two hours a day and then afterwards the boys should learn a trade at home, while the girls attend to home duties.

Luther emphasized the New Testament.

Religion was to be the foundation for all instruction. He emphasized the New Testament because of its relation to the development of Christian knowledge and character. After religion, Luther recommended mathematics and nature study. He had a partiality for history because it taught morality through men's lives and events, but history must not be tampered with, nor God's hand in it obscured. He believed that every school should have a library and that music was "one of the most beautiful and glorious gifts of God."

Ratich (1571-1635)

Ratich was one of the educational heirs of Luther. He believed:
- Everything should be taught in the natural order, from the easy to the more difficult.
- Only one thing should be learned at a time.
- The same thing should be repeated several times (directly opposite Charlotte Mason's pedagogy, see next chapter).
- Repetition—not memorization—is the teacher.
- All school books should be written on the same plan.
- The whole picture should be learned first before specific details.
- Everything taught should be by induction and experiment.
- Everything should be taught without coercion—the human understanding learns with pleasure all that it ought to retain.

Bacon (1561-1626), at the beginning of the seventeenth century, had opened unknown routes to scientific investigation. Now the focus was on the concrete study of reality—the living and fruitful observation of nature. It was necessary to ascend, step by step, from the knowledge of the simplest things to the discovery of the most general laws—the knowledge of things instead of the analysis of words.

Comenius (1592-1671)

Comenius—the Bacon of modern education—put into practice the pedagogy of Ratich. He wrote a large number of books, including two that were models for the later illustrated primers and readers such as *McGuffey's*. His phonetic system is similar to that used by most homeschoolers today. His system of grade levels is still evident also, corresponding to preschool, primary, secondary and college.

After age six, the children were to enter school. "The purpose of the people's school shall be that all children . . . may be instructed in that knowledge which is useful during the whole of life." Children were taught the mother tongue, arithmetic, geometry, singing, history, natural sciences and religion. Grammar was simplified—children needed examples, not abstract rules. Rules ought only to aid and confirm usage. The primary school contained a complete course of study—although remaining elementary—and was a whole and not just a beginning. This could be compared to American country schools at the beginning of the twentieth century, where one who finished eighth grade had a solid basic knowledge of various subjects.

Nature Study

In the place of dead books why should we not open the living book of nature? . . . To instruct the young is not to beat into them by repetition a mass of words, phrases, sentences and opinions gathered out of authors—but it is to open their understanding through things . . . .

Comenius demanded that the faculties be developed in their natural order—first the senses, then the memory, then the imagination; and lastly, the judgment and reason.

We must offer to the young, not the shadows of things but the things themselves, which impress the senses and the imagination. Instruction should commence with a real observation of things and not with a verbal description of them.

The Reformation was a breaking with authority in matters of religion, as the Baconian philosophy was a breaking with authority in matters of science; their joint effect on education was to subject matters of opinion, belief and knowledge to the individual reason, experience and observation. In the recoil from the intuition of the intellect sanctioned by Socrates, to the intuitions of the senses sanctioned by Bacon, education passed from extreme dependence on reflection and reason to extreme dependence on sense and observation.

➥ After reading this chapter, you may wish to go back and amend your Philosophy of Education. Add any new or amplified thoughts to your notebook.

11
Mining the Methods

I like the high quality vintage books . . . simple yet literary method of learning . . . since God provided, I chose to purchase. —June 24, 1998

Each homeschooling method has something to offer. Here we mine nuggets of "gold" from the best of a number of methods that are compatible with EasyHomeschooling. If you would like to know more about a particular method, see "Resources."

Unschooling

The best feature of unschooling is that your child can study whatever topics he is interested in. Because of this, he will apply himself more diligently to learning.

Is this a style of learning that Christians should consider? Jesus said in Matthew 11:30, *For my yoke is easy, and my burden is light.* But we are also commanded to teach our children His statutes. *All scripture is given by inspiration of God, and is profitable for doctrine, for reproof, for correction, for instruction in righteousness* (2 Tim. 3:16). Because there is no mention of school in the earliest Hebrew culture (see Chapter 10), I believe that the Hebrews were unschooled in every area except God's laws, commandments and statutes.

When state regulations specify that we must spend a certain number of hours at schooling, many of us feel compelled to spend all of this time in a very structured setting—no matter if we are destroying our relationship with our children and their desire to learn in the process! Unschooling would alleviate this pressure. I would agree that unschooling would be acceptable, if the schooling process includes a systematic study of God's Word, and that learning materials be available in abundance—such as those from the library. If you can purchase items related to your child's interests, so much the better, but this is not necessary if free or on-hand resources are used.

For more information, see the secular unschooling publications, ☞ *F.U.N. News* and ☞ *Home Education Magazine.*

Relaxed

Although some Christians are concerned that a relaxed approach is unbiblical, Mary Hood Ph.D.—author, speaker, editor and publisher of ☞ *The Relaxed Home Schooler's Newsletter*—believes that "You can loosen up and look more like a family without compromising your Christian beliefs."[1]

> *I definitely differentiate the "relaxed" method of homeschooling from unschooling because of my emphasis on underlying structure, including . . . Christian family structure, underlying time frame for the day, emphasis on long range goals and the role of the parent which definitely includes filling in perceived gaps along the way to those goals.*[2]

Mary tells how to get started if your child has recently been taken out of a school. The parent can tell the child that each day he must do something related to learning.

> *If the kids have no idea what you are talking about, you can give them suggestions: "You could read a book or write a story or a letter to Grandma, or do some work in your math book." I would also have a regular story time where I read interesting books to them. . . . By helping a child develop more responsibility for his own learning, you can help him develop self-discipline.*[3]

✔ Mary Hood says to assign classics when children are reading too many lower quality books. Written and oral communication skill is the primary prerequisite for college. She also recommends having students do term papers for college preparation.

The Moore Formula

Dr. Raymond and Dorothy Moore grandparented this method of study. The Moore Formula combines school with work and service, and garnishes it with a healthful, wise lifestyle. The Moores say that the most important qualifications for parents are warm responsiveness and a "fairly decent basic education."[4]

The Moore Formula is similar to unschooling in some ways. The Moores suggest the parent provide not workbooks, but plenty of time for the child to pursue his interests. However, they do not suggest that all assignments and formal work be eliminated altogether.

The Moores recommend no formal schooling until your child is eight or twelve, especially if a boy, and have been consistent in saying that all learning necessary to prepare for high school can be accomplished in only two or three years. They say that this delay and concentration will result in a more successful student. Although the Moores suggest that the parent wait to start formal schooling, they are in no way suggesting that the parent neglect to read to and respond to their children from their earliest age.

"Delay + Concentration = Success"

✐ I think the Moores make a good point. Consider this option. Determine when you will begin serious study and do concentrated, very disciplined tutoring during this two- to three-year period. You must first determine exactly what comprises a good education, and make your plan for those years. Previous to this period, let your child's life be filled with play, lots of read-alouds, independent reading, work, journaling, family business and perhaps a few scholastic endeavors (but not filled with video, computer games or TV!). Let him know early that when he reaches the designated age, formal schooling will begin. Should you use a curriculum's placement testing previous to formal schooling, you may find that much progress has been made without even trying, because of your informal literary foundation. (Accelerated Christian Education, for instance, uses placement tests.)

Moore Philosophy

The Moores say that spending more time with peers than parents before age eleven or twelve causes peer dependency. Children who feel needed, wanted and depended upon have the best self-confidence. The longer they are taught at home the higher this self-concept. Homeschooled students do develop the ability to think things through maturely and consistently from five to eight years earlier than conventionally schooled children.

Sensible and easy, proven to give great results, the Moore formula as described in ☞ *The Successful Homeschool Family Handbook* provides meat for every Christian homeschooler to "chew on" and "digest." This book provides a six-page summary of the Formula. The book not only arrests and stimulates, but also—more importantly— motivates to action. The bottom line: Be a loving, responsive parent. Respect your kids and look forward to an abundant harvest.

Moore Methods

✔ Rely on discussion and project learning, but don't neglect drill for mastery of basics. Ask "why?" and "how?" more than what, when, where and how much. Have fun with your children. Be a good example and warmly share fellowship with your children throughout the day. Be extremely selective in choosing materials or workshops. Make sure materials are easy to use.

Regarding discipline: We should have that first! The Moores suggest that we work on one habit at a time, encouraging those good ones already formed. Work on regularity and a schedule that is flexible. We must model to our children selfless, unconditional love.

Family industry and service are not electives. Teach service—first at home, then elsewhere. Share family management and family business. "Students who work with their hands develop common sense and practical skills, and do much better with their heads."[5]

✐ The above book is an EasyHomeschooling Top 10 book. See the entire list in ❀ *Easy Homeschooling Companion.*

The Robinson Curriculum

The Robinson Curriculum puts an end to the yearly task and expense of buying new materials. A one-time purchase provides all subjects for all children in all grades, even beyond high school. The twenty-two compact disks contain high quality vintage books that may be read on the computer or printed out. These valuable and hard-to-find books not only foster a love for reading, but can also transform a child's personality and behavior. With the Robinson Curriculum, all subjects are learned through reading, writing and arithmetic.

We were introduced to the Robinson Curriculum (RC) by a good friend who did a review (excerpt above) for our former newsletter. I was so impressed by the Robinson's firm literary basis and easy techniques that we purchased the CDs with the proceeds from selling used school items that we had accumulated. ✐ Zephi eventually completed her schooling at home at age sixteen entirely on her own by completing the RC booklist and doing advanced *Saxon* courses. (See more about Zephi, and her graduation speech in ❀ *Easy Homeschooling Companion.*)

The Robinson Curriculum consists of an easy schedule— math first, a one-page essay, and then reading for a number of hours. When we used Robinson, the children read independently from the booklist, while our family reading aloud was from other special vintage books.

Some children read for two hours or more, and some or all of the books can be read aloud. Along with the math lessons each day, a one-page essay may be done on what the child has read. Younger children may copy famous literature, the book they are reading . . . into a spiral notebook or journal. This teaches them all the necessary punctuation, sentence structure and spelling. Older children can do more essays and book reports, along with copywork. They can also write on their specific areas of interest in journals or in reports. The only other materials I purchase are used Saxon math—*which is the suggested math curriculum—and other titles my children enjoy that are not on the CDs but are in keeping with the vintage quality.*[6]

Dr. Robinson—a scientist—says that there is no need to dissect a frog to learn the circulatory system. I like this approach to science, and the method's literary focus in all subjects. The use of primary sources (writings by those who lived the history) make the course valuable. I also like the independent study techniques although there must still be a system of accountability. The biggest problem with this curriculum, in my opinion, is the temptation to neglect interaction, since it is a self-teaching method. I had to schedule in our read-aloud times!

The CD set that we had included the complete set of the 1911 *Encyclopedia Britannica,* the 1913 *Webster's Dictionary,* the original version of the *King James Bible,* plus nearly three hundred other scholarly and children's books. Also included for some of the books were vocabulary lists, exams and essay questions. The RC is costly, but not if divided out among a lot of years, or a lot of children, or both. You may purchase the Robinson CDs or get more information about this method, and other options for doing lower-cost, Robinson-*style* educating from ☞ **Home School Treasures.**

Charlotte Mason

Charlotte Mason was a British educator who lived and worked at the turn of the century. Her ideas had a great impact during her time and continue to influence an increasing number of educators today. Miss Mason believed that children should have a generous curriculum—characterized by nobility and forbearance, marked by abundance—with rich bouquet and flavor—the best of the best, and without limit. Miss Mason's books are also "generous," both in ideas and in words. Although rich in ideas, I feel her thoughts could have been communicated in less words. ✗ **Do as I did when reading her books, and use a highlighter to mine the many nuggets of gold.**

Much of the following is directly quoted from Miss Mason's *A Philosophy of Education*[7] and from back issues of *Parent's Review*. ☞ **The Charlotte Mason Research and Supply Company.**

Narration

Miss Mason said that children will be attentive to reading if interesting literary books are used, and if they know for certain that no second or third reading will be allowed. After the reading the child is to tell back the passage read, giving as much detail as he remembers. This is called narration.

> *Children must do the work for themselves. They must read the given pages and tell what they have read. . . . All school work should be conducted in such a manner that the children are aware of the responsibility of learning; it is their business to know that which has been taught. To this end the subject matter should not be repeated. . . . To allow repetition of a lesson is to shift the responsibility for it from the shoulders of the pupil to those of the teacher. . . . A single reading is a condition insisted upon because a naturally desultory [aimless] habit of mind leads us all to put off the effort of attention as long as a second or third chance of coping with the subject is to be hoped for.*

A Literary Feast

"The mind . . . has a natural preference for literary form"—as opposed to hearing a lecture of predigested material. Therefore "oral teaching was to a great extent ruled out; a large number of books on many subjects were set for reading in morning school-hours; so much work was set that there was only time for a single reading; all reading was tested by a narration of the whole or a given passage, whether orally or in writing." Any questions or comments were to be asked or stated only after the student's narration. With such a feast of literature, very little grammar teaching was needed.

Once children are allowed a due share in their own education . . . our chief concern for the mind or for the body is to supply a well-ordered table with abundant, appetizing, nourishing and very varied food, which children deal with in their own way and for themselves. This food must be served "au naturel," without the predigestion which deprives it of stimulating and nourishing properties, and no sort of forcible feeding or spoon feeding may be practiced. Hungry minds sit down to such a diet with the charming greediness of little children; they absorb it, assimilate it and grow thereby in a manner astonishing to those accustomed to the dull profitless ruminating [turning a matter over and over] . . . so often practiced in schools. . . . No rewards or punishments are necessary . . . students voluntarily, immediately, and perfectly give full attention to these lovely books. . . . Complete and entire attention is a natural function which requires no effort and causes no fatigue.

The teachers underrate the tastes and abilities of their pupils. . . . What they want is knowledge conveyed in literary form . . . give a child a few fit and exact words on the subject and he has the picture in his mind's eye, nay, a series, miles long of really glorious films; for a child's amazing vivifying imagination is part and parcel of his intellect.

The best available book is chosen and is read through perhaps in the course of two or three years. . . . No stray lessons are given on interesting subjects; the knowledge the children get is consecutive. . . . they know and write on any part of it [the day's reading] with ease and fluency, in vigorous English; they usually spell well. There are no revisions.

Miss Mason believed that the home should be a rich library. This library can be built, over time, without great expense: "Books . . . may be picked up at second-hand stalls with the obliterated names of half-a-dozen successive owners."

Among her suggestions for young children are *Andersen's Fairy Tales, Aesop's Fables, Pilgrim's Progress* and *Just So Stories* by Kipling; later *Rob Roy* by Scott, Goldsmith's poems, Stevenson's *Kidnapped,* Shakespeare and Homer—and for all ages—the Old and New Testaments, whereby children learn to know God.

We have a treasury of divine words.

But what sort of approaches do we prepare for children towards the God whom they need, the Saviour in Whom is all help, the King who affords all delight, commands all adoration and loyalty? Any words or thoughts of ours are poor and insufficient, but we have a treasury of divine words which they read and know with satisfying pleasure and tell with singular beauty and fitness. . . . By degrees children get that knowledge of God. . . .

History

I believe that Miss Mason would approve of autobiographies of famous people who lived and took part in history, such as those written by Benjamin Franklin, George Washington and Winston Churchill. She cautioned:

Not stories from history, but consecutive reading, say forty pages in a term, from a well-written, well-considered large volume which is also well-illustrated . . . [not pictures, but examples, incidents and anecdotes]. The work . . . is always chronologically progressive. . . . It is never too late to mend but may we not delay to offer such a liberal and generous diet of history to every child . . . as shall give weight to his decisions, consideration to his actions and stability to his conduct; that stability, the lack of which has plunged us into many a stormy sea of unrest.

Other Subjects

"Mathematics are to be studied for their own sake and not as they make for general intelligence and grasp of mind."

For art appreciation, works of the masters are studied, one artist at a time, six paintings per term. Miss Mason said that great paintings should not be copied lest the child loses reverence for the original, but that they should "illustrate favorite scenes and passages in the books read during the term." This, along with narration, shows just how much the child is comprehending from the passages read.

Books dealing with science . . . should be of a literary character . . . and we should probably be more scientific as a people if we scrapped all the text-books which swell publisher's lists. . . . The principles which underlie science are at the same time so simple, so profound and so far-reaching that . . . these principles are therefore meet subjects for literary treatment, while the details of their application are so technical and so minute as—except by way of illustration— to be unnecessary for school work or for general knowledge.

However, Miss Mason believed there was a place for field and laboratory work and encouraged nature study with notebooks in which the child sketched and wrote descriptions of what they were observing.

The Peaceful School

"Two conditions are necessary to secure all proper docility and obedience. Given these two, there is seldom a conflict of will between the teacher and the pupils."

Two Rules for Homeschool Peace

1) *The teacher . . . must act so evidently as one under authority that the children, quick to discern, see that they too must do the things they ought.*

2) *The children should have a fine sense of the freedom which comes of knowledge, which they are allowed to appropriate as they choose, freely given with little intervention from the teacher. They do choose and are happy in their work, so there is little opportunity for coercion, or for deadening . . . talk.*

☞ **The Classical Method**

Classical education was common in Britain and arrived in America with the colonists. Its focus is on using language effectively and persuasively. Classical education emphasizes Latin, logic, rhetoric and Christian worldview thinking.

Language

God chose to reveal Himself primarily through language—even prohibiting the use of images representing Him. A genuinely classical education:

. . . assumed an environment bursting with language, in stark contrast to our own more image-centered day. The classical and Christian mind was a mind surrounded by an ocean of language. Every day, all day, in family devotions, work, education, recreation, church and civil duties—language, as opposed to communication by images, governed experience . . . [and] produced minds and habits very different from those of a culture like our own.[8]

Language requires precise mental discipline (thought), whereas the visual promotes idle minds. Only mental discipline, acquired by literary learning, results in growth, intelligence and maturation—obviously lacking from many in an image-centered culture. For a truly classical mind, language should far surpass time spent with images. (Even fine art should be subordinate.)

Most homeschoolers have an obvious aversion to television, but by regularly providing their children with 'decent' cartoons and video games, [they] do nothing to encourage the habits of reading . . . [however] a classical and Christian perspective in education gives us a reprieve from such frenzy (entertainment, entertainment, entertainment). It reminds us to slow down, to read carefully, to meditate calmly, to work honorably.[9]

Classical education is more than just adding Latin or Greek to one's curriculum. Parents should educate simply for mastery in the basics of writing, reading and speaking. They should not complicate education with every course available nor should they be concerned with entertaining children.

"Classical education is about literature, history, languages and math." Abstract thinking in arithmetic and counting is important. A child does not need manipulatives. "Science . . . should be taught under the aegis of literature and history—we should read the great words of the great scientists."[10]

Not hard work, but discipline and attention.

Hard Work

It is said that the classical method takes "hard work." We all know that "reading" isn't hard work, but to take up a book and read takes discipline; to comprehend, takes attention. Beyond much reading— and more important—is quality reading. Although a purpose of classical education is to teach children to learn for themselves, this curriculum also says that children need to be taught, or led to an understanding, and that children cannot be taught literature that the parents have not read.

Classical education 1) conducts the child through the Trivium (grammar, dialectic, rhetoric), 2) is distinguished by the study of subjects such as Latin, logic, theology and rhetoric, and 3) recognizes that our children have been born into a Western culture and that this heritage should be imparted to them.

Two other uses of "classical" education should be rejected by evangelical Christians: 1) a return to the paganism of ancient Athens and Rome, and 2) the view of Thomas Aquinas that the ancient philosophy of Aristotle should be merged with Christianity.

Latin

Latin 1) provides an efficient way to learn the grammatical structure of English, 2) is the key to about fifty percent of English vocabulary, 3) is the key to all romance languages, 4) helps develop a precision of mind that is helpful in subjects such as science, and 5) appears frequently in the literature of Western culture. Latin should be studied first, as a springboard for Greek, since Greek is more difficult.

Latin can be taught from a book with no concern for pronunciation, because no culture today speaks Latin, and no one is certain of the original pronunciation. Although there are classical and ecclesiastical pronunciations, the simplest method is to say it as though it were English. The important thing is to maintain consistency in pronunciation.

Logic

An argument, in logic, is a reason for believing something and an answer to the question, "Why?" It includes two parts—a group of one or more premises and a conclusion. In logic, the student must first distinguish between the structure (skeleton, basic framework) of the argument, and its content.

"Formal logic can be seen as part of mathematics and logical thought should be encouraged in all subjects."[11]

Rhetoric

Aristotle asserted that rhetoric is necessary in order to be persuasive. Classical (oral) rhetoric developed in the Greco-Roman world and revived during the Renaissance and Reformation. Rhetoric is divided into five canons. The first three are applicable to all communication, including essay and letter writing.

The Five Canons of Rhetoric

1) *Inventio*—arguments, illustrations and content are developed.
2) *Dispositio*—content is arranged in advantageous order.
3) *Elocutio*—one considers how best to say it all.
4) *Memoria*—speech is memorized.
5) *Pronuntiatio*—speech is delivered.

Tota et sola Scriptura
All of and only Scripture

Christian education should not be just like secular education with prayer and Bible tacked on. Rather, the Bible must be at the very center of our schools—a hub, with all else revolving around it. Once again, we come face to face with our great responsibility to be the example:

> *[A child's] character is forming under a principle, not of choice, but of nurture. The spirit of the house is breathed into his nature, day by day. The anger and gentleness, the fretfulness and patience—the appetites, passions and manners—all the variant moods of feeling exhibited round him, pass into him as impressions and become seeds of character in him; not because his parents will, but because it must be so, whether they will or not. They propagate their own evil in the child, not by design, but under a law of moral infection. . . . The spirit of the house is in the members of the children by nurture, not by teaching, not by any attempt to communicate the same, but because it is in the air the children breathe. . . . Understand that it is the family spirit, the organic life of the house, the silent power of domestic godliness, working as it does, unconsciously and with sovereign effect—this it is which forms your children to God.*[12]

"[We] ought, by God's Spirit, to discipline ourselves and our children in the fruit of the Spirit, the testimony of faithful warfare. And most assuredly, we ought to live in unhesitating confidence that Christ has conquered the enemy."[13] *And having spoiled principalities and powers, he made a show of them openly, triumphing over them in it* (Col. 2:15).

To educate in a classical manner, you will have to collect materials from various sources. "As the task of educating yourself and your children continues and broadens, you will always have a need for more books." Try finish a book every week or two. ". . . A parent's vocation is to learn in order to teach."[14]

☞ The Principle Approach

The Principle Approach brings America's Christian and Biblical form of government into every subject, applying these principles to scholarship, character formation and self-government. The model of Christian character is Pilgrim character, with qualities of faith and steadfastness, brotherly love, Christian care, diligence and industry, and liberty of conscience. With the Principle Approach, the educator is to become a living textbook and a tutor. The parent must study diligently before being "qualified" to teach their children.

This curriculum is classical and Biblical and depends upon the providential view of history. Some of the techniques used are overviewing, researching, reasoning, relating, recording and a notebook approach. No details were given about these techniques in the materials I requested for review, nor were they explained when I made a personal call to the company. Although supposedly a high-quality program, some of the biographies promoted were poorly-written twentieth century publications. This a very expensive method (the suggested activities and materials listed below total approximately $700). Moreover, the materials about this "Approach" are unclear and emanate "education."

How to Begin, according to F.A.C.E.
(The Foundation for American Christian Education)

1) Get the 3 basic volumes
   - Noah Webster's *1828 Dictionary*
   - *Christian History of the Constitution*
   - *Teaching America's Christian History*
2) Get the *Noah Plan Program Notebook* and work through the "Self-Directed Seminar."
3) Attend a seminar.
4) Join and support F.A.C.E.
5) Work through the provided sample lesson worksheet.

An Easy Approach to the Principle Approach

1) Use a Bible.
2) Find and use an old *Webster's*. We have one from the 1800s that includes Bible references, like the one F.A.C.E. sells.
3) Study source documents, particularly messages and papers of the founders and presidents, such as John Quincy Adams.
4) Have your students do research and keep notebooks of their research. For instance, use one notebook for each person, president or period studied. Copy the scriptures that the action or words were based on. Reason whether the actions show Christian character.

☞ **Five In A Row**
Review by Terri Earl

Rather than writing her own curriculum, Jane Clare Lambert built unit studies around a carefully chosen group of the very best in children's literature. Each story is read five days in a row. In addition to enjoying the variety of illustrations and wonderful storytelling in these books, we are covering a wide range of topics. We have learned about cultures from faraway lands and times, memorized the elements of a good story and improved our own writing. We have also experimented with science, practiced art and music and had lots of fun with real-life math. Mrs. Lambert recommends working on one "subject" a day.

To begin, I stocked up on some art supplies, hung up a laminated world map and checked the card catalog at the library for available books. It takes me about fifteen minutes on the weekend to look through the coming lesson and choose which project(s) from each subject to work on. By using the local library, this system has been unbeatably affordable.

✔ I assign additional reading to the older children from our library of old and classic books. They often may choose which selection they read; then must write a report or summary of their selection. I check this for spelling and grammar. The older ones have also enjoyed independently researching, preparing and presenting science experiments for the entire family on the science subject of the week. FIAR is one simple book to guide lessons for the group. We have the fun and simplicity of working together on unit studies, without being intimidated by a huge guidebook.

FIAR covers all the things children are supposed to commit to memory in those early years, and all in a painless form. And it acquaints them with classic literature. They quickly get the idea that some of the best stories have been around for many years.

☞ Far Above Rubies
Review by Somer Gauthier

Far Above Rubies is a high school curriculum written by Lynda Coats. It covers the traits that every girl will need to become a godly woman and wife according to Proverbs 31, but does not neglect academic meat. FAR is a freeing curriculum—allowing you to do what is right for your family instead of what is right for others, bringing you and your eleven- to nineteen-year-old daughters on a closer walk with each other and with God.

Do what is right for YOUR family!

FAR lists many activities to give you options. One of the biggest mistakes I see new users making is thinking that they have to do everything listed under each subject. In our family, the girls do math, grammar, spelling and Bible in the morning and then in the afternoon I read aloud from the suggested reading. We enjoy this so much as I find out what they are reading individually, giving us plenty to talk about. Then they do research, bake, sew, cross-stitch, do art and music, play learning games or work on their notebooks.

Some families use several notebooks—journal, spelling, vocabulary, history, home economics, science and so forth, while others have none. Heather and Amber use three notebooks each.

1) Their main notebook is divided into history, English and Bible. This is where they keep reports, guidelines on composition and special Bible verses.

2) Next is a journal. I will sometimes read aloud a chapter from a certain book and then ask them to write in their journal what their thoughts were on that chapter.

3) The last one is a free notebook. Amber's is on pregnancy and babies. Heather's is on animals. When ever they find a pamphlet, picture or article, they put that into their notebook. If they write a report on it, they will add it. It is amazing how good and large these notebooks are getting. This is their favorite school project since they are permitted to make decisions about it, and work on it entirely by themselves.

Far Above Rubies is a unit study designed to train young ladies to become the godly wives and mothers who will impact the next generation for the Lord Jesus Christ. It is the primary emphasis of this course to train our daughters for, and encourage them in their likely vocation of wife and mother, making them helpers to their husbands, nurturers of children and keepers of the home. However, due to the uncertainty of life and God's command to be prepared like the ant, we also help these young women gain a well-rounded education and learn marketable skills. . . . There is also a companion volume for boys called Blessed is the Man that was written specifically to correlate with FAR. This allows families with both boys and girls to use many of the same materials while achieving the proper generic emphasis for each student.[15]

12
Building a Business

Thank you Lord, for growing my business. —July 4, 1998

You have unique talents! As your children grow, your confidence and skills will also grow. When your children are about to depart the "nest," you might have a leading to begin planning (with your husband's blessing of course) for ministry or business. With the children home, there is the possibility of a family business. Your young adults may need guidance for their future life-choices. "The Right Business," below, is especially appropriate for them as they begin to walk in God's will for their lives, and in the "gifts" that He has given them.

I have rewritten this chapter for all three of the above-mentioned groups—family, young adults and the empty-nest mom (which you are not *now,* but will be someday!).

A Warning

✐ I will never recommend starting a business to any mother of children under age thirteen or fourteen. You have enough to do. More importantly, your children *really* need your undivided mothering. You have a very special family and you know that yours is the best profession. Many working mothers have told me that they would prefer to be home with their families! If you are home now, thank God every day. He has already given you His best job. Even with the challenges, it is a far better life.

Do not start a business unless you are absolutely sure that God is leading you in that direction. Perhaps your business idea is for a later time in your life—when your children are grown and living on their own. You do not want to look back with longing on the family that grew much too fast while you were taking care of business. However, if you are already working at a job or business, there are easy ways to combine that with homeschooling, which I will share later in the chapter.

God provides for our families, especially those families that have chosen to do His work of raising their children for Him. Nine times out of ten, mothers do not have to earn extra income. Actually, unless God is definitely leading you otherwise—your family will be more blessed financially if you *do not* work or start a business.

If you have considered these warnings and listened for the Lord's still small voice, when you have waited and received His direction, when you are sure that this is His leading for you and your family, when your husband is in complete agreement—then, and only then—begin a business. A business often distances a mother from her family, unless it is a family business.

✐ Family Business

A family business is a whole different matter! If you are sure that a business idea can put each of the children to work with you, a business idea is a good thing. The children must be involved in the business on a daily basis—make sure that they are old enough to be involved and that you have specific jobs planned for them to do with you. They must work at it as often or nearly as often as the parents do. It will do them a world of good and bless the entire family. (See more about the value of family business in Dr. Raymond Moore's books.)

When I think about family business, I think about a small grocery or retail store or an income-producing farm. There are farms in our area where the children do not take part in the work, because of public school activities, or the general laziness of today's children—perhaps both. It was not like this a few decades ago. These landed patriarchs end up calling *our sons,* knowing that they are hard workers and available.

Many homeschoolers have opened curriculum businesses, with the children doing packing, shipping and toting to curriculum fairs. I cannot recommend this type of business though—it seems to me that the market is saturated.

Selling a tangible product—as opposed to writing or other individual creative work—would be a better family business. With a product, there are always simple tasks to do such as packaging, organizing, labeling, hauling and sometimes—depending on the child's age—selling.

In our business, the girls and Andy have done excellent proofreading, while Ezra, Eli and Andy still do heavy work such as unloading cases of books into our warehouse. They have also all helped at curriculum fairs.

It takes money to make money!

Businesses often—and often for a long time—cost more than they make. Instead of adding to the family's budget, you may drain it even more by starting a business. Break-even point is when business expenses are are finally met by business income. Because of this startup period, many businesses don't make it. You must be prepared. Do not make the mistake of going into business when you have immediate needs or limited funds. Do not attempt to "open your doors" until you have more than the most money that you think you will need to take care of your business "baby" as well as the other babies in your family for a number of years. Home businesses are the least expensive to start, but there are always some expenses. The largest expenses for home businesses are equipment, expansion, advertising and—if you sell a product—inventory. It is better not to start at all than to have to quit after spending many years and many dollars promoting a business. *And Jesus said unto him, No man, having put his hand to the plow, and looking back, is fit for the kingdom of God* (Luke 9:62).

Business Readiness

During your time of preparation—which could be months, or even years—your tasks are to:

1) Save specifically for your business.
2) Decide what kind of business to start.
3) Research business, generally and specifically.

While you putting away money for business start-up costs, you can be "homeschooling" yourself. Your library has an abundance of business books, magazines and videos—possibly even some about the particular business that you are considering. Some libraries also have scanners, printers and other equipment. I actually started our business at the library using their computers and printers.

Take advantage of every business learning opportunity that you can. If you can afford to go to conferences, do so. Buy books if you can. Check out business videos or buy them. Do all the learning you can before "opening your doors"—you may not have time for it after! *To every thing there is a season, and a time to every purpose under the heaven* . . . (Eccl. 3:17). See "Resources" for suggested ☞ **Business Books.**

The Right Business

Here is another notebook idea to pinpoint exactly what kind of business would be best for you—what ministry or career to pursue if a young adult. It is ideal if you have a large chunk of time available; however, you may take a break and return to this project later. When returning, you will probably have thought of other things you can add.

➡ Gather several pages of notebook paper and a good pen. You are going to list everything you have ever done—not just the jobs you have had, but every single thing that you can remember doing. For example: sawing wood, watching TV, going down the river on a raft, playing a game. It might help to think about different "hats" you have worn and then list what was done done in that capacity. To keep your papers more orderly, use headings, such as "Homeschool Teacher." Then list activities done under that heading. As you start writing, your thoughts will start flowing and more and more things will pop into your mind. Just a few words for each listing is sufficient, but make sure you put down everything that you can think of. Ask a close friend or family member if they can help with these recollections. I filled seventeen pages! Although time-consuming, this is foundational for picking the perfect business or career.

Now look over your list and circle all of those things that you really enjoyed doing. Then next to each circled listing, put an "A" for those things you do well, a "B" for those things you do not do well, and a "C" for those things that you do not do well, but would like to improve—and can improve—such as typing speed.

You may wish to list separately all the items that you circled, especially the "A's" and the "C's." Study your lists. The fun begins! You will see a pattern emerging. You will discover that you have enjoyed similar tasks and disliked similar tasks. As a result of this brainstorming session, you will probably see a business, ministry or career emerging that will tie together all of your skills and talents and desires and be the best choice for you.

✐ In *Write It Down, Make It Happen,* Henriette Anne Klauser says to write things as if they had already happened. While this doesn't apply to the above project it does apply to your dreams and goals in this area of business. She says that fiction becomes non-fiction, giving several examples in her book of that happening.

Other Preparation

"Find a need and fill it." Good advice. Find out if there is a market for what you plan to do. You can post questions related to your product or business service on the appropriate bulletin boards. I have written articles based on input gathered in this manner.

Write a business plan. Although most often used for the purpose of getting business financing (loans), a business plan can be a map that will help you get to where you want to go in business. To learn basic accounting systems get ☞ *Small Time Operator.* Look for this book at your public library.

After you have accumulated startup costs and a store of knowledge, and after carefully considering the warnings above, plunge in! A family friend, who had been involved in many businesses, gave me some simple and yet profound advice. He said, "Just do it!" One can talk and talk, prepare and dream but, for those who are sure of the Lord's leading, this is the best advice. If you start wisely—in your home, without debt and with savings—there is little financial risk involved, therefore little to be apprehensive about.

As your business awaits a burst of success, do not get discouraged if there are days, weeks, or even months when the money does not come in. Proverbs 21:5 says, *The thoughts of the diligent tend only to plenteousness; but of every one that is hasty only to want.* So just keep at it, when you are not busy with your family. Do a little every day and the harvest will come.

Whew! You made it through the startup period. You have become wildly successful! But now you will be wildly busy as well, which will take you away from your family even more. Or you will be forced to to grow and expand—hire others or move, or both—which will eliminate the hominess of a home business and take you even farther away from the home circle. However, if you are already a "sole" proprietor, you can explore new options and tasks to draw your children into the business with you.

Write detailed job descriptions for each child.

Marketing

Marketing includes advertising, but much more than advertising. When a homeschool book seller gives a talk at a convention or a local support group, she is marketing. When two companies swap flyers to use for inserts in the packages they send out—they are marketing. When you write a personal letter to a customer or potential customer, you are marketing. Marketing can be loosely defined as anything that is done that could result in sales. There are free marketing activities.

If you have a unique product or idea, and can write reasonably well, you can market by writing articles. Most publications would rather let you add a tag line about your business than pay you. And those few lines may be more profitable than being paid for the article, especially if the publication has a large circulation.

You can buy an inexpensive brochure holder and ask related businesses to display your brochure. (Be sure to check back regularly to refill.) Place posters on bulletin boards everywhere, and check back regularly and re-post if necessary.

Think bartering. Always offer something besides cash in return for what you want. You may be surprised at how many businesses are willing to do this. Offer to speak to groups whose members might be interested in your expertise. Many times you can sell at this time. If not, pass out simple information sheets with contact information. My favorite book on general marketing is ☞ *Guerrilla Marketing* by Jay Levinson. It includes many low-cost ideas. ✎ Look for books on marketing for your specific field. I have several on book marketing, each packed with more ideas than I find time to use.

You may choose to do internet marketing. This alone can be quite effective. There are various bulletin boards where you may post free ads for your product or service. We send an email newsletter, notification of new titles and of new additions to our stock of vintage ☞ **Exceptional! Books.**

Networking

Business networking is connecting and interacting with others with the motive that they become future customers, or a future help to one's business. Networking was one thing I skipped over in the business books I read. The concept seemed so self-serving! What homeschooling mom would have the time to form the relationships and join the clubs, anyhow? However, the Lord showed me His networking system. *Neither are your ways my ways, saith the LORD* (Is. 55:8).

The world's way of networking has selfish goals. God's way of networking is primarily for mutual edification and growth through fellowship. *Iron sharpeneth iron; so a man sharpeneth the countenance of his friend* (Prov. 27:17). As much as I hate even the thought of worldly networking, I love godly networking!

Along with fellowship, friendship and counsel, my blessings have included free advertising, free publicity, endorsements from well-known people, free subscriptions, bartered subscriptions and five times the going rate for articles! All of these blessings were given with no strings attached. They were a token of the unconditional love of Christ that He wants us to walk in. These examples have just made my desire to bless others stronger.

Godly networking enabled me to receive godly counsel. My primary counsel has come from God himself through His Word—which is perfect, profitable, and wonderful—but never before had I experienced the multitude of counselors talked about in Proverbs! *Where no counsel is, the people fall: but in the multitude of counselors there is safety. Without counsel purposes are disappointed: but in the multitude of counselors they are established* (Prov. 11:14, 15:22).

In the multitude of counselors there is safety.

The Lord has provided a miracle mix in "my" network. Our products may be similar but because of Him, we are not competitors. We have each been in business approximately the same time. We are learning together and yet we have our own special niche. It is so like our Father to direct us in such an individual and yet parallel way.

Another difference between worldly networking and godly networking is that in the Lord's networking, these relationships are not sought after. *But seek ye first the kingdom of God, and his righteousness; and all these things shall be added unto you* (Matt. 6:33). When He brings these people to you, do what He would have you to do and be a blessing. *But this I say, He which soweth sparingly shall reap also sparingly; and he which soweth bountifully shall reap also bountifully* (2 Cor. 9:6).

Advertising

Advertising can be very expensive, and often it seems those dollars are tossed into the wind. Your product must be a mid- to high-cost item to merit expensive advertising in a consumer magazine. These ads are best left to established businesses whose products do sell, and who have a regular higher income with an established customer base.

✗ Contact the publications that you consider best for your particular product and ask for their advertising rate sheets. Ask these questions first about each publication: What is the circulation? (How many readers are there?) Ask yourself, "Are these readers people who would be interested in my product?" Then:

1) Pick the absolute best *one* publication for your product.

2) Decide on a small display ad or a classified ad.

3) Study other ads and write yours based on what response you want. One of our best ads was a longer classified written in narrative. I believe it attracted people because it sounded more personal.

4) Include in your start-up costs enough funds to cover three to twelve months of insertions in this one publication.

5) Start with one insertion. If proceeds from this ad cover the cost, make a longer, three to six month commitment with the same publication.

If you made money off your ad, don't make the mistake of spending it before re-advertising, or sales may trickle to a stop. After your tithes and offerings, as a Christian business person, advertising should be first. Keep it simple. If a publication's ads are making money, stay with it. Don't make the mistake of scattering your money to the four winds—to a multitude of different publications. Later when you are ready to expand, you can add one publication at a time.

Again, make sure that God is leading you to start a business. Most work—even creative work—is so empty in eternity's light. And yet the work put into our children will hold forever. What greater joy than spending the precious few years with those nearest our hearts.

Homeschooling while Working

Even if you work outside the home, you can homeschool. If you are working at a job or business twenty hours a week, another twenty at homeschooling would be only equivalent to a full time job. Even with working forty hours a week at a job or business, you can still teach your children at home. If you read a few hours each night, your child's skills would surpass those of public-school students, whose parents have to spend the evenings reteaching the things the children haven't learned at school.

Those of you who have a seasonal business or just work certain months of the year may schedule school for the months that your business is slower, or for the months that you are not working. A twelve-month schedule would be ideal for some. Spend about three hours each evening, and four or five on Saturday at schooling. You may spend even less time at school, depending on 1) your state's requirements, 2) whether your child can do independent study, and 3) how much informal learning you plan to do.

The weekend would be ideal for hands-on learning along with workbooks, reading and field trips. Workbooks and flash cards work well for math. You may wish to supplement your science reading with experiments. There are many books available on experiments that can be done with simple materials.

On the Lord's Day you could study the Bible—read, dictate, memorize and recite to honor the Lord, learning language arts at the same time. Read creation science materials. Study church history.

See "Starting Up," Chapter 2, for details on what and how to teach. Be sure to use subject combining (Chapter 6) to save time. This is one of the most important techniques for busy working moms.

Child Care

You and your husband might be able to stagger your working hours. He works while you are home; you work while he teaches and cares for the children; or visa versa. If you are using the schools as a care giver, here are some suggestions:

1) Time share care with a friend—while one of you works, the other teaches one or two subjects to the children. While you are working, your older children could be either doing some of their schoolwork, or helping your friend with the younger children.

2) Your older child could be working, possibly as an apprentice in a chosen field.

3) Your older child could be babysitting and teaching your younger children.

4) Your older child could be doing school work and keeping up the house.

5) Your younger children could be at a church day care or relative's house. Your children are being taught life skills as well as academics so they will be a blessing, not a burden, to others.

Is your child enrolled in a private school? Homeschooling could save you money. With EasyHomeschooling you can provide a high quality education for much less. With so many money-saving helps and ideas, you may find that you can live without an extra income and become a full-time homeschooling mom.

Tips from Working Mothers

First, be sure that you are on God's schedule and following His suggestions. Downscale. If you go shopping twice a week, start going once. If once a week, go once every two weeks. Stay home. Organize. All you really need is a Bible. Be judicious about cutting the fat out—in every area of your life: Curriculum. Possessions. Activities. Try alternating days for business and school.

Shari Henry
Author of Homeschooling: The Middle Years

Allow children complete access, including them in all chores, meal prep . . . filling their tanks emotionally. Then, insist on a quiet time for each person and get busy. Ask the Lord continually for guidance.

Deb Deffinbaugh
☞ *The Timberdoodle Company*

So how do we do it all in schoolwork? By insisting on a system of accountability for each child. We have found that children will accomplish far more and learn far better when we stop hovering over them. Children sincerely desire to have as much control as possible over their lives, and this is a wonderful way to introduce them to the adult world of responsibilities and consequences.

Anne Olwin,
☞ *Artist and art teacher*

Prepare ahead of time for deadlines. Have snacks and other activities on hand for young ones. Involve the children—sure it's easier to do it yourself, but you're missing an opportunity for training them in life skills and godliness if you fail to involve them. It saves time in the long run. Laugh! Keep a good sense of humor—everything is more difficult and takes longer if you don't. ✐ *Five years later, Anne adds for this new edition:* It amazes me that the Lord has richly given me the desires of my heart both with my family and with my art business. The importance of faithfulness in raising and homeschooling my children cannot be overstated. In that season my home business was small, but I learned to make the most of my time and I honed my skills. Now that the children are grown, I reap the rewards of a close strong family that loves the Lord and the art business is exploding in a way I could not have envisioned then.

Leese Griffith
Writer, small business owner

I try to combine errands whenever possible, and "work" mainly during afternoon quiet time and after the boys go to bed. When a big job comes in and I am juggling too much, we slack off a bit during the day and Daddy does more in the evenings—like listening to our oldest read, or doing projects.

Catherine White
Former editor of An Encouraging Word

Fit school in—don't be rigid. Sometimes fit work in. Simplify house-work and cooking, extracurricular activities, life—eliminate TV, stay home and run errands on one day. Don't collect knickknacks that clutter your home and life by having to take care of them.

Shelli Owen
Formerly of The Homeschool Supply House

I. Overlap tasks.
  • Bedtime stories and literature
  • Counting games, identifying colors, shapes and letter sounds, while walking or driving
  • Scripture reading and devotionals with meal times
II. Simplify life
  • Fewer things to take care of—smaller house, fewer store bought toys for kids
  • Organization
  • Sharing of house and yard work (chores)
III. Keep priorities. Most important are:
  • God
  • Family
If I do these things, then everything else seems to fall into place—if not immediately, eventually.

Nancy Greer
☞ *F.U.N. News and Books*

Include your children in your work if you can. They will learn lots of important skills that many adults don't have. Our children have learned that if the business phone rings, they need to do a quiet activity. We make sure that crayons, paper, etc. are in a child-reachable spot. Let your child do as much as is safe. Our son can prepare his own breakfast and lunch if needed. He's proud of it, and he's learning important skills. Also—you're going to have to decide what's important. If you work, something else is going to have to give. Maybe the laundry piles up some, or you don't dust as often. You may be able to do everything for a while, but your sanity or health will suffer eventually.

✐ *Beth Nieman*
Librarian, Carlsbad, NM

On days when I work, I cook supper right after breakfast! I work evenings, so I'm not home for supper. My family likes casseroles, chilis, lasagna, stews and similar items. I bake the main course in the morning and start a loaf of bread in my bread machine, timing it so that the bread will be done when my family is ready for supper. Sometimes I prepare salad or dessert as well. I put a portion of whatever I've made aside to take with me for my dinner break, and put the rest in the refrigerator for my family to heat and eat. I still get to enjoy cooking, we save money by eating out less, my family gets a hot meal every night, and there's no pressure on my husband to fix dinner when he is tired after work.

13
Sailing through High School

I began "keeping credits" for the girls' high school records.
—August 20, 1997

For EasyHomeschoolers high school is a smooth transition with more of the same and only minor differences. There will be more and greater literature, more extra-curricular activities, more service, and more emphasis on excellence. High school is also the time for deeper individual studies and for exploring ministries, careers and colleges. The previous chapter, "Building a Business," provided a detailed a notebook plan to help your young adults discover what calling they are best suited for.

By this time your child should have ➦ listed his dreams, goals and the steps needed to meet those goals. (See instructions throughout this book.) Some of these goals may have been met by now. With goals in place, learning will also fall into place as the step lists are worked in the direction of your young adult's goals.

It is crucial that the students themselves make these plans, rather than their parents. Unless the teens have had significant input into the planning phase, they will generally be recalcitrant when it comes to putting forth the required effort.[1]

Antique and Classic Books

College is a means to an end and not the end in itself. Your child should have goals beyond college. If college is a step to those goals, they should begin preparation while in high school.

A priority for high school is that you guide your child into more depth in literature. Great literature produces great minds. For high school, use more of the same, and even greater selections.

Now—along with a thorough study of God's Word—your student may read Shakespeare, *The Federalist,* Machiavelli, Dumas and the Greek classics. Your high schooler may now read authors such as Darwin, because your young adult needs to know opposing thought. Just make sure that God's Word has—and has had—the preeminence in your home. One thing to remember is that we are never old enough for debasing literature that sullies the mind and heart!

For fifteen- to eighteen-year-olds, Charlotte Mason suggested Pope's *Essay on Man,* Carlyles *Essay on Burns,* Goldsmith's *Citizen of the World,* Thackeray's *The Virginians, The Oxford Book of Verse,* Plutarch, and the Old and New Testaments. Miss Mason also said that for this age, ". . . some definite teaching in the art of composition is advisable, but not too much, lest the young scholars be saddled with a stilted style which may encumber them for life."[2]

Round out your young adult's studies with the lighter classic authors such as Steinbeck, Austen, Stevenson, Scott and Alcott—if they haven't been read yet.

See ✐ *Easy Homeschooling Companion,* "Loving Literature," for learning techniques and more recommended books and authors.

Reading Aloud

Don't think that your students are now too old for read-aloud times. Reading aloud can stand alone, but now you may wish to do more to to encourage a Christian worldview, to understand deeper writing such as poetry or to actually practice English or speech skills. Your students are now able to think more deeply about a subject and discuss it more thoroughly. A Christian worldview can be imparted partly through these discussions. Present questions that require reflection. Some questions may not even have an answer. However, these questions stimulate the thought process, which is what we want to cultivate in our children.

Cultivate your student's thought process!

Independent Study

Your students can do independent study from antique books. Always have a system of accountability. Do not neglect to enforce completion of assignments. Expect papers—summaries of what they have read. Do not let your students go one day with an overdue assignment. If they are allowed to miss deadlines and not finish projects, they will not learn the valuable traits of completing what they have begun. Term papers and reports can be done using antique books for reference. Most have a wealth of interesting facts and ideas.

With a bedrock of the solid content of antique books, your children will graduate with sound, thoughtful minds, able to discern between good and evil. *Butter and honey shall he eat, that he may know to refuse the evil, and choose the good* (Is. 7:15).

Science & Math

Continue with a good math program such as *Saxon*. Our girls began algebra in seventh grade and used the *Saxon* texts throughout high school. *Key to Algebra* should be used before *Saxon* algebra to facilitate comprehension of algebraic concepts. Our younger daughter, Zephi, did *Key to Algebra* before Algebra 1, and was whizzing through the *Saxon* books with no problems whatsoever, whereas Jessica—who hadn't done *Key to Algebra* first, had problems. But *Key to Algebra* cannot stand alone. After completing the workbooks, Zephi could not complete the *Saxon Algebra 1* test. (*Key to Algebra* is a workbook series, widely available from homeschool catalogs.)

For science, your high schooler can study scientists and their discoveries. Investigate and duplicate the scientific experiments of noteworthy scientists for lab work. Require reports about these lab experiments. Have them dig deeper and thoroughly investigate each theory, including their opinions and thoughts. Always use God's Word as the final authority.

Keeping Credits

Although high school is a smooth and often unnoticible transition from the early grades, there is a difference. Colleges expect transcripts (a record of the high school classes and grades given for each). Therefore, in high school, any and all activities should be recorded. These will include cleaning, cooking, washing vehicles, teaching a little sister and writing a term paper. Even the most ordinary activity will be credited to "Life Skills" or "Home Economics."

You do not need to keep credits when you use a text—such as math—because completion of the book fulfills the required credit hours per year. But do keep track of time spent on activities related to that subject. Reading and reporting on a book titled *The History of Algebra,* for instance, may be needed for speech credits when computing is done in the senior year. Record everything in case you need to fill in gaps later. Don't forget art and Shakespeare videos, field trips and so on!

It works best to have the children keep the credits themselves, although you may need to remind them until it becomes habit. Check regularly to see that it is being done.

➼ Use a large three-ring binder with index dividers for each subject. Notebook paper "timesheets" for each subject will be placed before their reports or other school papers in that section of the notebook. You may have several timesheets for each subject. Start with one for each.

How to Calculate Credit Hours

- Make separate "timesheets" for each of the topics your high schooler covers (such as Global Studies) and place them in the proper section of the notebook. Choose the topic heading that will most likely fit the activity. A the top left of the notebook paper write the topic heading such as Global Studies, Home Economics, or Life Skills. Label it "Other," if you do not know where to put it. Later it may be easier to place these unusual activities where they need to go.
- On the top right, place a subheading such as "England," if the topic is Global Studies. (On the "Other" time-sheet you do not have to note a subheading.)
- Draw a narrow column on the right side of the paper.
- Draw two narrow columns on the left. Leave most of the space in the center for a description of the activity. If necessary, you may use several lines for each activity.
- On the right, record the actual hours spent on each individual activity or class, using decimals instead of fractions for portions of the hour, to make totaling the hours easier at the end of the year.
- In the center section of the page, tell what was done at that time.
- In one of the columns to the left, if applicable, place a reference number such as "GS-3" (Global Studies, Paper 3) which will also go on any paper or report related to that activity.
- In the second column on the left side of the paper, alongside the above reference number, insert a grade from that paper or report.
- At the end of each year, add up—or have your son or daughter add up—the actual hours spent at each subject.
- List the total hours on another "master chart" for that year. All subjects can be on one paper on this sheet. Along with listing hours actually spent per subject, you should average the grades given on reports or other projects for that subject, and record a final grade for each subject.

- Now you can find the credit hours earned for that year. In a classroom setting, much time is wasted as the teacher gives out instructions, hands out worksheets or makes other announcements. The schools uses 160 hours for each credit. Since homeschooling is so efficient, we can use 140 hours or possibly even less to compute our credits. Divide the actual hours by 140 (140 actual hours = 1 credit hour). How many credit hours should you have? 20-32 is customary for graduation; 5-8 per year. To get an exact figure of credits needed for graduation in your state, check with a local high school or your state's department of education. If your child has a particular college in mind, you should check with them as well. Along with grades and credit hours, the transcript must have the student's date of birth and date of departure from school. You can find sample or blank transcripts on the Internet.
- Staple or clip the corresponding timesheets to the report papers that your student has written, subject by subject. Place the stack in a nine-by-thirteen manila envelope. If necessary use one envelope per subject. Label the outside of envelope with the subject (or topic if you have many, many papers), school year, and total hours for that subject. Then file all the envelopes away in a box or use a large rubber band to bind them together with a copy of your master chart of total credits for that year. Keep in a safe place! Especially keep your "master chart" safe, and keep duplicate copies—perhaps in several formats—paper, computer and disk.

Credit keeping is a continual activity because each day is made up of many activities. When reviewing your child's annual credit hours you may find them short. Don't be concerned. You will balance things out in the next years of high school by focusing more on the areas where more credits are needed. Here are the credit hours required for high school graduation in one state. The credit hours required for the advanced course (college preparatory) follow the standard chart.

Standard High School Course

4.0 English
4.0 Social Studies (W. History, A. History, Gov., Economics)
4.0 Mathematics (Include Algebra I & Geometry)
4.0 Science (Include Biology I and any Physical Science)
1.0 Physical Education (or approved substitute)
0.5 Health Education
0.5 Computer Applications
5.5 Electives

Advanced Course

All of the above, plus:
2.0 Foreign Language (all the same language)
0.5 Fine Arts
Algebra II and Trigonometry are added to the math requirements with the same total hours. Electives are reduced to 3.5

College

More and more colleges recruit the independent-thinking, well-prepared homeschool student. Jessica began sending for college catalogs at fourteen after reading, ☞ **Home School, High School and Beyond.**

Open Admissions Colleges

Open admissions colleges admit anyone over eighteen or with a high school diploma. Standardized college admissions testing is not required, nor is any particular high school course selection. Grades in high school are not relevant. Students who have not taken an academic preparatory program in high school may need to complete some high school level courses before taking college courses for credit toward a college degree. Such courses are usually available as remedial classes and may be taken at the college.

✐ Rarely, if ever, is one asked for the actual diploma with the granting institution's seal. It is usually only a question on job applications. "Do you have a diploma or an equivalent?" The GED is the diploma option we have used for all of our children. We avoided having to have a transcript (for some) by having the child leave school before applying for the GED. With Zephi we had more red tape because she was under the preferred age. Contact your Adult Basic Education board to find the requirements for your state. Sometimes this group is affiliated with a city or community college. In Nebraska, the students are well-prepared for the test by GED classes. A no-cost ceremony and a reception is also provided!

Selective Admissions Colleges

Applicants to selective colleges must meet the criteria set by that particular college. Schools with selective criteria may look for students with high grade-point averages, rigorous academic preparation, high scores on the standardized college admissions tests, strong personal qualities and evidence of achievement. Some colleges are more selective than others. Selective colleges may require applicants to submit high school grade-point averages and rank in class, scores on standardized admissions tests (SAT or ACT) and letters of recommendation. Some may require a personal interview, and some may be particularly interested in the student's extracurricular activities.

✐ Get SAT prep books and software from your public library or purchase *The SAT College Preparation Course for Christian Students*.

Life Skills

Perhaps more important than knowledge or a college education, are the skills that your adult children will use almost every day. These can be learned throughout your child's homeschooling years, but should be mastered in high school, if not previously. Girls can learn sewing, cooking, finances and hair cutting. Young men—alongside their father, if possible—can learn auto upkeep, household repair and so on.

Our first skills class was "Quilting." I began by assigning a small antique book which included the history of quilting. Then I assigned study of the passages about Dorcas (Acts 9). Next the girls looked through quilting books and designed patterns. Their grandmother (a real Dorcas!) gave us many quilts, afghans and appliqued quilt tops, so the girls were given the option to use one of her quilt tops or start from scratch.

Another life skills unit could be "Cooking." Your child would plan menus for a week, shop, find scriptures on food and memorize them, cook all the meals for a week—including the side dishes and breads, create a recipe, write a paper on cooking techniques, and help with bulk cooking for the freezer. ☞ *Dinner's in the Freezer!* is a guide-book for this big family project.

Your young men could do similar studies, along with learning the more masculine skills. Boys should learn housekeeping—they may be bachelors! If so, they will need to know how to cook and keep their homes clean and neat. Should they marry, they should know how to do household chores to help as needed. At the very least, learning housekeeping will teach them not to make the job harder for their wives.

Life Skill Class

1) Find scriptures that relate to the topic. Memorize, meditate.
2) Research the subject.
3) Report, including what knowledge or steps are needed to become skilled in that area.
4) Learn the skill through hands-on training and experience. Let this be acquired over a long period of time. A week or two will not train for life. Better to have your young adult take over your finances or car care for the year, or until leaving home.

A Word About Courtship

Not only is there too much focus on "romance" in the world, there is too much focus on "courtship" in homeschooling circles. The premise of courtship is that the young adults are totally ready to marry—the young man being able to support a wife. Why, then, stir up these thoughts before their time by exploring the topic? We made it a habit to never joke about boyfriends or girlfriends. When the topic arises, we speak of the fact that there is a time for everything in one's life and that this is not the time. The best preparation is a godly education, a godly example and life skills well learned. A good resource for marriage preparation is the workbook ☞ *Relationships, Pure & Simple.* There are so many problems in marriages nowadays. Our children need all the help they can get. Most importantly, pray for your children and their future spouses when your children are young and keep it up. Prayer will provide someone who will be a blessing, and God's perfect will for them.

14
Abiding in the Vine

My ministry now is my four little ones . . . and my husband.
—January 3, 1989

I have put this most important chapter last, so it would linger with you as you finish this book. John 15:4 says, *Abide in me, and I in you. As the branch cannot bear fruit of itself, except it abide in the vine; no more can ye, except ye abide in me.* The Lord has brought us to this task because—as always—he wants us to depend entirely on Him.

God Teaches the Teachers

For Ezra had prepared his heart to seek the law of the LORD, and to do it, and to teach . . . (Ezra 7:1). Note the order. First God teaches the teachers. As we yield daily, He will teach and train us to teach our children. Of primary importance is a daily time with the Lord. *I love them that love me; and those that seek me early shall find me* (Prov. 8:17).

During these quiet times the Lord will give spiritual, physical and mental strength for our many tasks. Studying His Word to find out how He wants us to live our lives will motivate us to do what He wants us to do. Allowing the Holy Spirit to fill us with gentleness, patience and consistency will qualify us to teach our children. *The servant of the Lord must not strive; but be gentle unto all men, apt to teach, patient . . .* (2 Tim. 2:24). *He that ruleth over men must be just ruling in the fear of God* (2 Sam. 23:3).

You Have a Helper

Be encouraged. You have Someone who is willing to come and give aid no matter what the need. The Holy Spirit is your helper—God's gift to you . . . *whom God hath given to them that obey him* (Acts 5:32). The Holy Spirit will give you help in every area of your life. He is always ready to assist those who stay attuned and ask in faith. *For he shall deliver the needy when he crieth; the poor also, and him that hath no helper* (Ps. 72:12). *I will instruct thee and teach thee in the way which thou shalt go: I will guide thee with mine eye* (Ps. 32:8). Perhaps you are attempting to do too much—is all that really necessary? He shall . . . *gently lead those that are with young* (Is. 40:11).

Help with Curriculum

How do I find the books that we use? I'm sure the Holy Spirit directs me to them! How else can I explain that perfect book to supplement our study, lying directly in front of my eyes on the rack at the library? How *perfect* that the day's historical overview ended at the gold rush, when my son just happened to get two books from the library on gold mining! What about the open book on my desk that reminds me of yet another historical figure that I want to investigate, but had forgotten? We Christians know that there are no coincidences in life, but a mighty God . . . *a very present help* (Ps. 46:1), who is ready to intervene for us no matter what the need!

Help to Lighten Your Load

Who I am, and even the fact that I am alive today is because He has been my help. Who I will become will be the result of His help.

Turn to God first before going to anyone else for help. Don't make the mistake of looking to man for answers that only God can give! The Lord will show you what you can do to lighten your load. Is your mind stayed on him? *Give us help from trouble: for vain is the help of man* (Ps.108:12).

"I have chosen thy precepts."

Are you forgetting to put Him first? Neglecting your Bible or quiet time? You must make time if you want His peace in the midst of the busyness. *Let thine hand help me; for I have chosen thy precepts* (Ps.119:173).

Are you praying, waiting and expecting answers? Or are you "standing in faith" for the worst and showing it by your actions and words? *Our soul waiteth for the LORD: he is our help and our shield* (Ps. 33:20). Don't forget that our mighty God is so desiring and able to help! *Let us therefore come boldly unto the throne of grace, that we may obtain mercy, and find grace to help in time of need* (Ps. 124:8). *Our help is in the name of the LORD, who made heaven and earth* (Heb. 4:16).

More than Conquerors (Rom. 8:37)

There may be days when you cry like a baby, because you have been everything but the godly, loving mother that you are supposed to be. Surprise! The devil hates homeschooling! He hates you! He hates your kids! Remember he's out to kill, steal and destroy! But God has promised us all we need.

Who is Responsible?

We wrestle not against flesh and blood, but against principalities, against powers, against the rulers of the darkness of this world, against spiritual wickedness in high places (Eph. 6:12). We need to recognize who is at the center of problems, and we need to continually keep it in mind, because our enemy continually *walketh about, seek-*

ing whom he may devour (I Pet. 5:8), so we need to continually be on guard. One of his sneaky tricks is making us forget that he is at the bottom of the mess! When strife rears its ugly head, don't blame yourself. Don't blame your kids! Don't blame your husband! When we recognize the devil as the antagonist in each instance, we are on our way to victory—because we know that he was conquered once and for all at Calvary! What seems to be defeat in our lives is only a lie.

Submit to God

Submit yourselves therefore to God. Resist the devil, and he will flee (James 4:7). Commit to submit. We overcome evil with good (Rom.12:21). When we submit to God and do good we are resisting the devil. You can find out what He wants you to do from the Bible—especially the New Testament. He will let you hear His still, small voice, if you are willing to listen. When he does, decide that you will submit and begin by doing that one thing. *You can do all things through Christ* (Phil. 4:13).

Pray without Ceasing

Pray without ceasing (1 Thess. 5:17). *Watch and pray, that ye enter not into temptation: the spirit indeed is willing, but the flesh is weak* (Matt. 26:41). Continually bathe your family in prayer. Pray every moment your mind is not occupied. Pray in the Spirit when it is, or at least maintain a quiet attitude of prayer and submission. Total dependence on God is important: His way—not ours.

Quiet Time

Don't neglect a daily quiet time. Spend at least one hour early each morning with Jesus—not with videos, Christian TV, devotionals or books—but with Him. Spend this time in his Word and in prayer. The poetic form of the *Authorized King James Version* has enabled me to recall many verses without actual memorization work.

Pray the Word

Pray and speak the Word all through the day. The Word is God's creative power. The book of Genesis tells what happened when "God said." Pray it when the devil sends negative thoughts or actions your way. "All my children are being taught of the Lord and great is the peace of my children." (Is. 54:13) "Thank you, Lord, that I have peace not as the world gives but as you give." (John 14:27)

This is not a gimmick! It will not work if you haven't planted the Word in your heart, for out of the abundance of the heart, the mouth speaks. (Matt. 12:34) But as your mouth continually speaks His Words, they will be created in your heart for *faith cometh by hearing and hearing by the Word of God* (Rom. 10:17).

A Power that Enables

But ye shall receive power, after that the Holy Ghost is come upon you: and ye shall be witnesses unto me both in Jerusalem, and in all Judaea, and in Samaria, and unto the uttermost part of the earth (Acts 1:8). God gives us a power to do the things that we cannot do otherwise. Homeschooling—being a witness to our children—is one of these things for some of us. I have experienced a measure of this "fullness" before and know that it is extraordinary—everything just falls into place the way it should! But it doesn't just come automatically. We must totally depend on and yield to the ways of God; an empty vessel, allowing the Holy Ghost to inhabit us and work through us.

God has made you a unique individual. If there is a struggle in your school, it could be that you are trying to fit someone else's style. *For my yoke is easy, and my burden is light* (Matt. 11:30). Throw off the shackles! Break the chains! With God's help and EasyHomeschooling, you can draw closer to your children as you learn in freedom and joy! What sweet relief!

Sunday's "Mother"

Billy Sunday was raised an orphan after his father died in the Civil War. After a stint as a professional baseball player, he was saved through a woman's preaching at Pacific Garden Mission in Chicago. He then spent an impeccable life turning multitudes to Christ and society to godly values. Prohibition was largely the result of this one man's widespread, bold and down-to-earth preaching. He speaks directly to us in the following sermon excerpt.[1]

The Task of Womanhood

All great women are satisfied with their common sphere in life and think it is enough to fill the lot God gave them in this world as wife and mother. I tell you the devil and women can damn this world, and Jesus and women can save this old world. It remains with womanhood today to lift our social life to a higher plane.

Mothers, be more careful of your boys and girls. Explain the evils that contaminate our social life today. I have had women say to me, "Mr. Sunday, don't you think there is danger of talking too much to them when they are so young?" Not much; just as soon as a girl is able to know the pure from the impure, she should be taught. Oh mothers, mothers, you don't know what your girl is being led to by this false and mock modesty.

Don't teach your girls that the only thing in the world is to marry. Why, some girls marry infidels because they were not taught to say, "I would not do it." A girl is a big fool to marry an infidel. God says, "Be ye not unequally yoked with unbelievers."

I believe there is a race yet to appear which will be as far superior in morals to us, as we are superior to the morals of the days of Julius Caesar; but that race will never appear until God-fearing young men marry God-fearing girls, and the offspring are God-fearing.

What paved the way for the down fall of the mightiest dynasties—proud and haughty Greece and imperial Rome? The downfall of their womanhood. The virtue of womanhood is the rampart wall of American civilization. Break that down, and with the stones thereof, you can pave your way to the hottest hell, and reeking vice and corruption.

Warning

You women can make a hell of a home, or a heaven of a home. Don't turn your old Gatling-gun tongue loose and rip everybody up and rip your husbands up, and send them out of their homes.

A Mother's Responsibility

As the Nile queen said to Moses' mother, "Take this child and nurse it for me." That is all the business you have with it. That is a jewel that belongs to God, and he gives it to you to polish for him, so he can set it in a crown.

"Take the child and nurse it for me, and I will pay you your wages." God pays in joy that is fire-proof, famine-proof and devil-proof. He will pay you, don't you worry. So get your name on God's payroll.

"Take this child and nurse it for me, and I will pay you your wages." Then your responsibility! It is so great that I don't see how any woman can fail to be a Christian and serve God.

"Take this child and raise it for me, and I will pay you your wages." Will you promise and covenant with God, and with me, and with one another, that from now on you will try, with God's help, to do better than you ever have done, to raise your children for God?

Mothers of Great Men

> The mother of Nero was a murderess, and it is no wonder that he fiddled while Rome burned. The mother of Patrick Henry was eloquent, and that is the reason why every school boy and girl knows, "Give me liberty or give me death." Coleridge's mother taught him Biblical stories from the old Dutch tile of the fireplace. Susanna Wesley held her children for God, "By getting hold of their hearts in their youth and never losing my grip." The ideal mother is the product of a civilization that rose from the manger of Bethlehem.

The ideal mother abides in the Vine.

Authors and Poets

These can be read by—or read aloud to—children in older or younger age groups. Most are classics or heirlooms, but not all have been reviewed.

1st to 8th Grades
The Bible: *King James Version*

Authors
- Louisa May Alcott: *Little Women* and others.
- James Baldwin: *The Story of Roland, Old Greek Stories*
- Thomas Bulfinch: *The Legends of Charlemagne*
- John Bunyan: *Pilgrims Progress*
- John Burroughs: *Birds and Bees, Sharp Eyes*, other papers
- D.M. Craik (Miss Mulock): *Adventures of a Brownie*
- Charles Dickens: *A Christmas Carol, Pickwick Papers,* others
- Oliver Goldsmith: *The History of Little Goody Two Shoes*
- Nathaniel Hawthorne: *Tanglewood Tales, A Wonder-Book*
- Victor Hugo: *Les Miserables*
- Washington Irving: *The Sketch Book, Tales of a Traveller,* others
- Charles Kingsley: *The Heroes*
- Rudyard Kipling: *The Day's Work, The Jungle Book, Just So Stories*, others
- Jack London: *The Call of the Wild*
- John Muir: *The Boyhood of a Naturalist*
- Helen Nicolay: *The Boy's Life of Ulysses S. Grant*
- Francis Parkman: *The Oregon Trail*
- Beatrix Potter: *Peter Rabbit* and others
- Walter Scott: *Redgauntlet*

- Ernest Thomson Seton: *Animal Heroes, Live of the Hunted,* others
- William Shakespeare: *A Midsummer Night's Dream*
- Henry van Dyke: *The First Christmas Tree, The Story of the Other Wise Man*
- Kate Douglas Wiggin: *The Birds' Christmas Carol, The Story Hour,* others
- Laura Ingalls Wilder: *Little House on the Prairie,* others
- W.B. Yeats: *The Hourglass* and other plays

Poets
- Katharine Lee Bates: *The Ballad Book*
- William Blake: *Songs of Innocence*
- Robert Browning: *The Pied Piper of Hamelin*
- Lewis Carroll: *Through the Looking Glass*
- H.W. Longfellow: *Collected Poems*
- T.B. Macaulay: *Lays of Ancient Rome*
- Christina Rosetti: *Sing-Song*
- R.L. Stevenson: *A Child's Garden of Verse*
- Alfred Tennyson: *Collected Poems*
- J.G. Whittier: *Collected Poems*

9th to 12th Grades

The Bible: *King James Version*
Basic Documents of American History

Authors
- Dante Alighieri: *The Divine Comedy*
- Aristotle: *Politics and Poetics*
- Austen: *Pride and Prejudice*
- Charlotte Bronte: *Jane Eyre*
- Thomas Bulfinch: *The Age of Fable*
- Cellini: *Autobiography*
- Crane: *The Red Badge of Courage*
- Defoe: *Robinson Crusoe*
- Dickens: *A Tale of Two Cities*

- Emerson: *Essays*
- Benjamin Franklin: *Autobiography*
- Machiavelli: *The Prince*
- Melville: *Moby Dick*
- Milton: *Paradise Lost* and *Paradise Regained*
- Hawthorne: *The House of the Seven Gables*
- Homer: *The Iliad* and *The Odyssey*
- Plato: *The Republic*
- Plutarch: *Lives of Ten Noble Greeks and Romans*
- Scott: *Ivanhoe*
- Shakespeare: *The Complete Tragedies, The Complete Comedies*
- Thoreau: *Walden*
- Tolstoy: *Ann Karenina*
- Twain: *The Adventures of Huckleberry Finn*

Poets
- Francis Bacon
- Robert Browning
- Robert Burns
- Lord Byron
- William Cowper
- Oliver Wendall Holmes
- Ben Jonson
- John Keats
- Charles Lamb
- John Milton
- William Shakespeare
- Percy Bysshe Shelley
- William Wordsworth
- H.W. Longfellow
- Alfred Tennyson
- J.G. Whittier

Jessica's Favorites

Jessica, our eldest, is now twenty-one and a bride. She provided this list for the first edition when she was seventeen.

Fiction

- Louisa May Alcott: *Little Women* (Civil War period)
- James Boyd: *Drums* (American Revolution)
- Esther Forbes: *Johnny Tremain* (American Revolution)
- Charles Dickens: *The Tale of Two Cities* (French Revolution)
- Lloyd C. Douglas: *The Robe, The Big Fisherman* (Time of Christ)
- Alexandre Dumas: *Count of Monte Christo, Edmund Dantes*
- G.A. Henty: *In the Reign of Terror* (French Revolution)
- Victor Hugo: *Les Miserables, The Hunchback of Notre Dame*
- C.S. Lewis: Narnia series (Christian fantasy)*
- Baroness Orczy: *The Scarlett Pimpernal* (French Revolution)
- Jane Porter: *Thaddeus of Warsaw* (Polish Revolution)
- Henryk Seinkiewicz: *Quo Vadis* (1st Century)
- Sir Walter Scott: *Ivanhoe* (Middle Ages)
- Shakespeare: *The Merchant of Venice* (Renaissance)
- Elizabeth G. Speare: *The Witch of Blackbird Pond, The Bronze Bow* (Am. Revolutionary period, Time of Christ, respectively)
- Lew Wallace: *Ben Hur* (1st Century)

Poetry

- Rudyard Kipling: *If*

Non-Fiction

- Dixy Lee Ray: *Environmental Overkill*
- Joshua Harris: *I Kissed Dating Goodbye*

Another opinion about the Narnia series:
These books . . . introduce children to a world of magic, witchcraft and demonic creatures. . . . I would not have my children read these stories . . . nor recommend them to anyone. Although, to most . . . . . . seems to be a creative story, at best it is a very poor allegory of the true spiritual realm. . . . —Caren Cornell, Home School Treasures

Course of Study

One does not have to study any particular topics in any particular grades. When in doubt, do things sequentially:"What happened first in history?" "What was discovered first?" "What in science was first?" "What was written first?" You may use the following for your scope and sequence—especially for the lower grades—or design your own plan. Add topics such as Music and Art, if you like. This does not necessarily fulfill any college or graduation requirements. For many more topics to choose from see World Book's *Typical Course of Study* in the parents' section of their site: ***www.worldbook.com.***

1st Grade

Bible

- ❏ Read aloud from Bible story book for overview
- ❏ Daily systematic Bible times (read through little by little)
- ❏ Memorization of shorter key scripture verses
- ❏ Establish Sabbath keeping
- ❏ Start repeating prayers with parents

Social Studies

- ❏ Local and family history
- ❏ Simple geographical terms
- ❏ Making and reading a simple neighborhood map

Science

- ❏ Nature study
- ❏ Animals, including birds and habitats
- ❏ Seeds, bulbs, plants, flowers
- ❏ Grouping and classification

Language Arts

- ❏ Phonics
- ❏ Enunciation and pronunciation
- ❏ Reading practice (only after mastery of phonics)
- ❏ Creating stories and poems—parent writes down
- ❏ Narration after parent reads
- ❏ Basic punctuation and capitalization
- ❏ Beginning handwriting

Health and Safety

- ❏ Establish habits: hygiene, including dental
- ❏ Exercise and rest
- ❏ Nutrition
- ❏ General safety rules

Mathematics

- ❏ Counting and writing to 100
- ❏ Beginning addition and subtraction facts to 5 or 10
- ❏ Concepts of equality and inequality
- ❏ Using 1/2 and 1/4 appropriately

2nd Grade

Bible

- ❏ Student begins reading from simple Bible story books
- ❏ Scripture memorization
- ❏ Family Bible times
- ❏ Begin individual Bible reading and quiet time
- ❏ Pray with parents, pray own prayers

Social Studies

- ❏ Holidays ☞ **Mantle Ministries** holy-day tapes
- ❏ Acquiring food and food sources
- ❏ World history overview
- ❏ Basic geography: oceans, continents
- ❏ Map use

Science

- [ ] Nature Study
- [ ] Earth and sky
- [ ] Sun, moon, planets
- [ ] Simple constellations
- [ ] Exploring space

Language Arts

- [ ] Reading silently and aloud
- [ ] Alphabetizing, dictionary guide words
- [ ] Handwriting
- [ ] Copywork
- [ ] Narration

Health and Safety

- [ ] Maintain or establish habits: cleanliness, dental
- [ ] Basic food groups
- [ ] The Christian's supernatural gift of health and safety (Deut. 28:61; Gal. 3:13; Psalm 91)

Mathematics

- [ ] Counting, reading, writing to 1,000
- [ ] Counting by 2's, 5's, and 10's
- [ ] Addition and subtraction facts to 20
- [ ] Basic multiplication and division facts
- [ ] Weight, length, volume, shape, temperature, time, calendar, charts, graphs

3rd Grade

Bible

- [ ] Scripture memorization
- [ ] Family Bible times
- [ ] Bible reading and quiet time
- [ ] Pray at meals and other times as asked
- [ ] Ministry to community with parents

Social Studies

- ❏ American biographies
- ❏ Local and national geography and topography
- ❏ Flat maps

Science

- ❏ Nature study
- ❏ Plants and animals of the desert
- ❏ Plants and animals of the sea
- ❏ Common birds, trees, flowers
- ❏ Forest plants
- ❏ Conservation

Language Arts

- ❏ Reading silently and aloud
- ❏ Dictation, narration, copywork
- ❏ Dictionary skills
- ❏ Beginning cursive writing
- ❏ Writing short, original stories and poems; editing, proofreading

Health and Safety

- ❏ Maintain or establish habits: cleanliness, dental
- ❏ Care of eyes and ears
- ❏ Proper balance of activities
- ❏ The body (Ps. 139:14)
- ❏ Nutrition

Mathematics

- ❏ Reading and writing numbers to 99,999
- ❏ Beginning Roman numerals
- ❏ Rounding numbers
- ❏ Addition and subtraction facts to 25
- ❏ Multiplication and division facts to 100
- ❏ Mastery of math facts: flash cards or other drill

4th Grade

Bible
- ❏ Ministry to community with parents
- ❏ Scripture memorization
- ❏ Family Bible times
- ❏ Bible reading and quiet time
- ❏ Pray independently and with family
- ❏ Establish Bible journaling: recording thoughts, verses, word studies, prayers and direction from God.

Social Studies
- ❏ State history
- ❏ Continents and climatic regions
- ❏ Time zones
- ❏ Using a globe

Science
- ❏ Nature study
- ❏ Insects, mammals, plants, reptiles
- ❏ Environment of the local region
- ❏ Earth and its history
- ❏ Oceans and the hydrosphere
- ❏ Air and water pollution

Language Arts
- ❏ Telephone manners and skills
- ❏ Making and accepting simple social introductions
- ❏ Summarizing simple information
- ❏ Cursive handwriting
- ❏ Simple outlining
- ❏ Developing skills in locating information
- ❏ Writing a report
- ❏ Narration, dictation, copywork

Health and Safety
- ❏ Maintain habits: cleanliness, dental
- ❏ Skeletal and muscular systems
- ❏ Care and proper use of the body
- ❏ Principles of digestion
- ❏ Substance abuse

Mathematics
- ❏ *Saxon* Math 54

5th Grade

Bible
- ❏ Scripture memorization
- ❏ Family Bible times
- ❏ Bible reading and quiet time
- ❏ Pray independently
- ❏ Continue Bible journaling
- ❏ Ministry to community with parents

Social Studies
- ❏ Exploration and discovery
- ❏ Settlement
- ❏ Revolutionary period
- ❏ Democracy's principles and documents
- ❏ U.S. geography, national resources

Science
- ❏ Animal and plant classification
- ❏ Bacteria
- ❏ Human body

Language Arts
- ❏ Silent and oral reading
- ❏ Homonyms, homophones and homographs, synonyms and antonyms
- ❏ Using a thesaurus

- ❏ Spelling
- ❏ Plurals and possessives
- ❏ Cursive handwriting
- ❏ Preparing a simple bibliography
- ❏ Writing and editing own compositions
- ❏ Using study materials: keys, tables, graphs, charts, legends, library catalogs, index, table of contents, reference materials, maps

Health and Safety
- ❏ Dental hygiene
- ❏ Public works: water, sewage
- ❏ Care of the eyes
- ❏ Nutrition and diet
- ❏ Elementary first aid

Mathematics
- ❏ *Saxon* Math 65

6th Grade

Bible
- ❏ Scripture memorization
- ❏ Family Bible times
- ❏ Bible reading and quiet time
- ❏ Pray independently
- ❏ Continue Bible journaling
- ❏ Ministry to community with parents

Social Studies
- ❏ Pioneers, westward movement
- ❏ Industrial, cultural and geographic growth
- ❏ Transportation and communication
- ❏ North and South America
- ❏ Citizenship and social responsibility
- ❏ War between the States
- ❏ Map and globe skills

Science

- ❏ Electricity and magnetism, electronics
- ❏ Sound, light and heat
- ❏ Energy: solar, nuclear, etc.
- ❏ Properties of water
- ❏ Light and color
- ❏ Simple and complex machines

Language Arts

- ❏ Types of literature
- ❏ Using roots, prefixes and suffixes
- ❏ Sentence structure, diagraming
- ❏ Cursive handwriting
- ❏ Writing and editing own compositions
- ❏ Types of writing: narration, description, exposition, persuasion
- ❏ Simple note taking
- ❏ Using reference books and indexes
- ❏ Using electronic reference materials
- ❏ Discerning author's worldview

Health and Safety

- ❏ Personal appearance, hygiene
- ❏ Exercise and fitness
- ❏ The health professions
- ❏ Systems of the human body
- ❏ Human reproduction

Mathematics

- ❏ Saxon 76

7th Grade

Bible

- ❏ Ministry to community with parents
- ❏ Continue with other Bible learning, etc.

Social Studies

- ❏ World History
- ❏ World trade and resources
- ❏ World geography
- ❏ Advanced map and globe skills

Science

- ❏ Composition of the earth
- ❏ Rocks, soil and minerals
- ❏ The earth's movement
- ❏ Conservation
- ❏ Ecosystems, ecology, environment
- ❏ Climate and weather

Language Arts

- ❏ Literature
- ❏ Planning and producing dramatizations
- ❏ Clauses and phrases
- ❏ Compound sentences
- ❏ Writing and editing descriptions, reports, journals, and letters
- ❏ Note taking and outlining
- ❏ Extending reference skills: atlases, directories, encyclopedias, periodicals, on-line information services, CD-ROMs and other electronic reference material
- ❏ Library organization

Health and Safety
- ❏ Good grooming and posture
- ❏ Dental health
- ❏ Healthy habits and lifestyles
- ❏ Exercise and fitness
- ❏ Circulation and respiration
- ❏ Antibiotics
- ❏ Personal and public safety
- ❏ Accident prevention

Mathematics
- ❏ Saxon Math 87

8th Grade
Bible
- ❏ Ministry to community with parents
- ❏ Continue with other Bible learning, etc.

Social Studies
- ❏ Current events
- ❏ Parties and politics
- ❏ Reconstruction to WW II
- ❏ National geography

Science
- ❏ The universe and Milky Way
- ❏ Astronomy
- ❏ Space and space travel
- ❏ Atmosphere
- ❏ Air pressure

Language Arts
- ❏ American poets and storytellers
- ❏ Spelling mastery
- ❏ Infinitive, participle, gerund, predicate nominative, predicate adjective, direct and indirect object

- ❏ Kinds of sentences and their parts
- ❏ Functions of sentence elements

Health and Safety
- ❏ Grooming
- ❏ The body's utilization of food
- ❏ Types and functions of foods
- ❏ Substance abuse

Mathematics
- ❏ *Saxon* Math Algebra 1/2

9th Grade

Bible
- ❏ Ministry to community
- ❏ Continue with other Bible learning, etc.

Social Studies
- ❏ Community, state and national government
- ❏ Political parties and elections
- ❏ Elementary economics
- ❏ Labor and management
- ❏ Modern history, post WW II
- ❏ Democracy vs. Communism

Science
- ❏ Scientific nomenclature
- ❏ Lab techniques and safety
- ❏ Scientific classification
- ❏ Scientific method

Language Arts
- ❏ Parable and allegory
- ❏ Interpretation of literature
- ❏ Effective discussion techniques and questioning skills
- ❏ Preparing a speech

- ❑ Public speaking and debate
- ❑ Foreign words used in English
- ❑ Grammar
- ❑ Fundamentals of composition

Mathematics
- ❑ *Saxon* Algebra I
- ❑ Personal and family math

10th Grade

Bible
- ❑ Ministry to community (state)
- ❑ Continue with other Bible learning, etc.

Social Studies
- ❑ Creation through the Reformation
- ❑ Classic literature of the periods studied

Science
- ❑ Biology, including microscopic life
- ❑ Photosynthesis
- ❑ Cells
- ❑ Genetics and heredity
- ❑ Environmental issues

Language Arts
- ❑ Novel, short story and essay
- ❑ Poetry: lyric and the sonnet
- ❑ Distinguishing between fact and opinion
- ❑ Persuasion and argumentation
- ❑ Public speaking and debate
- ❑ Dictionary skills
- ❑ Grammar
- ❑ Techniques of writing
- ❑ Writing short stories, poetry and plays
- ❑ Writing term papers

- ❏ Constructing footnotes

Mathematics
- ❏ Saxon Algebra II

11th Grade

Bible
- ❏ Ministry to community (state, nation)
- ❏ Continue with other Bible learning, etc.

Social Studies
- ❏ American history

Science
- ❏ Chemistry

Language Arts
- ❏ American literature
- ❏ Poetry
- ❏ Critical and evaluative reading
- ❏ Vocabulary development
- ❏ Grammar
- ❏ Editorial, journalistic writing
- ❏ Writing term papers
- ❏ Proofreading symbols
- ❏ Use of Reader's Guide and other reference aids, both print and electronic

Mathematics
- ❏ *Saxon* Advanced Math

12th Grade

Bible
- ❏ Ministry to community (state, nation, world)
- ❏ Continue with other Bible learning, etc.

Social Studies

- ❏ Government: national, and comparative
- ❏ Current events, politics, missions, law
- ❏ National business and industry
- ❏ International relations
- ❏ Democracy vs. Communism
- ❏ World interdependence, problems and issues
- ❏ English history

Science

- ❏ Physics
- ❏ Electronics
- ❏ Nuclear energy
- ❏ Atomic structure

Language Arts

- ❏ English literature, including Shakespeare
- ❏ Literary, social, and political heritage of England
- ❏ World literature
- ❏ Writing term papers

Mathematics

- ❏ Saxon Calculus
- ❏ Computer literacy
- ❏ Family finances

Sample Scope and Sequence

Most concepts can be covered the EasySchool way, with much reading and writing. This is a sample only. Design your own special scope and sequence!

Grade 3

I. **Social Studies**
- A. Bible
- B. Church history
- C. Geography
    1. European
    2. African
- D. Review Egypt, Greece, Rome, Middle Ages
- E. Renaissance, Reformation, beyond.

II. **Science**
- A. Meteorology
- B. Men and women of science

III. **Language Arts**
- A. Reading
    1. The Bible
    2. *McGuffey's* readers
- B. Writing
    1. Stories
    2. Poems
- C. Penmanship
- D. Speech

       1. Enunciation

       2. Memory work

   E. Mechanics of language

       1. Spelling

       2. Grammar

       3. Punctuation

IV. *Health*

   A. Organs

   B. Prevention and safety

   C. Men and women of health

V. *Mathematics*

   A. *Practical Arithmetics* text

   B. Facts drill

   C. Story problems

Class Schedule Planner

Class Schedule Planner				Year:		
Time of Day	Monday	Tuesday	Wednesday	Thursday	Friday	

Notes:

Resources

Preface

God's Gardener
PO Box 95
Boelus NE 68820
308-996-4497
Fax: 308-996-9104
info@easyhomeschooling.net
www.easyhomeschooling.com
FREE Copywork, checklists, articles, newsletter.

F.U.N. Books
1688 Belhaven Woods Court
Pasadena MD 21122-3727
Fax/Voice 410-360-7330
Orders: 888-386-7020
FUN@FUN-Books.com
www.FUN-Books.com

Home Education Magazine
PO Box 1083
Tonasket WA 98855-1083
Orders: 800-236-3278
HEM@home-ed-magazine.com
www.home-ed-magazine.com

The Successful Homeschool Family Handbook
The Moore Foundation
Box 1
Camus WA 98607
360-835-5500
Fax: 360-835-5392
Orders: 800-891-5255
generalinfo@moorefoundation.com
www.moorefoundation.com
Better Late Than Early, School Can Wait, etc.

Chapter 2

Home School Legal Defense Association
PO Box 3000
Purcellville VA 20134-9000
540-338-5600
Fax: 540-338-2733
info@hslda.org
www.hslda.org/laws/default.asp

Home School Manual
Gazelle Publications
11560 Red Bud Trail
Berrien Springs MI 49103
800-650-5076
info@gazellepublications.com
www.gazellepublications.com

Dover Publications, Inc.
31 E 2nd St
Mineola NY 11501-3852
Fax: 516-742-6953
info@doverpublications.com
www.doverpublications.com

Simply Phonics

Shoelace Books
3086 Juhan Road
Stone Mountain GA 30039
www.shoelacebooks.com

Scholastic Inc.

800-246-2986
www.scholastic.com

Home School Treasures

450 Golden Nuggett Way
Maysville GA 30558-3802
706-652-2258
hstreasures@juno.com
www.hstreasures.com

Keepers of the Faith

404 S Mine St
Bessemer MI 49911
906-663-6881
Fax: 906-663-6885
sales@keepersofthefaith.com
www.keepersofthefaith.com

Cindy Rushton

Rushton Family Ministries
1225 Christy Lane
Tuscumbia AL 35674
256-381-2529
time4tea@hiwaay.net
www.cindyrushton.com

Chapter 3

Saxon Publishers
2600 John Saxon Blvd.
Norman OK 73071
800-284-7019
info@saxonpublishers.com
www.saxonpublishers.com

Chapter 4

Don Aslett's Cleaning Center
311 South 5th Avenue
PO Box 39
Pocatello ID 83201
208-232-6212
Fax: 208-235-5481
www.cleanreport.com

Chapter 5

Course of Study
Scope and Sequence
Class Schedule Planner
All located in this section of the book.

Chapter 6

National Gallary of Art
National Lending Service
2000B South Club Drive
Landover MD 20785
202-737-4215
Fax: 202-789-3246
www.nga.gov/education/education.htm

Kids Art

PO Box 274
Mt Shasta CA 96067
530-926-5076
Fax: 530-926-5076
info@kidsart.com
www.kidsart.com

Cindy Rushton

See Chapter 2, above.

Dr. Raymond Moore

See The Moore Foundation, "Preface," above.

Simply Phonics

See Chapter 2, "Starting Up" above.

Chapter 7

The Lester Family

PO Box 203
Joshua Tree CA 92252
760-366-1023
info@lesterfamilymusic.com
www.lesterfamilymusic.com

Home School Treasures

See address above, Chapter 2.

Mantle Ministries

228 Still Ridge
Bulverde TX 78163-1878
830-438-3777
Fax: 830-438-3370
info@mantleministries.com
www.mantleministries.com

Exceptional! Books

See God's Gardener, above under "Preface."

Practical Arithmetics

Keepers of the Faith, address above.

Chapter 8

The Successful Homeschool Family Handbook

See above, "Preface."

Chapter 9

Bob Jones University Press

Greenville SC 29614-0062
800-845-5731
Fax: 800-525-8398
bjupinfo@bjup.com
www.bjup.com

Hobby Lobby

Visit your local store.

Art Teaching Books

- *Drawing Textbook*
- *Drawing with Children*
- *The Beginning of Creativity*
- *Usborne Guide to Drawing*

National Gallery of Art

See above, Chapter 6, "Combining Subjects."

Typical Course of Study

www2.worldbook.com/parents/course_study_index.asp

Math Writing Books

By Marilyn Burns

Math and Literature

The I Hate Mathematics! Book

Amazon.com, bookstores, libraries. Other resources by Marilyn   Burns are availble from ETA/Cuisenaire, 800-445-5985, www.etacuisenaire.com

Chapter 10

The Charlotte Mason Research & Supply Company

PO Box 758

Union ME 04862

www.charlottemason.com

Chapter 11

F.U.N. Books

See "Preface" above.

Home Education Magazine

See "Preface" above.

The Relaxed Home School

PO Box 2524

Cartersville GA 30120

relaxedhomeschool@juno.com

www.relaxedhomeschooler.com

The Successful Homeschool Family Handbook

See above, "Preface."

Exceptional! Books

See "Preface" above.

Home School Treasures

See address above, Chapter 2.

The Charlotte Mason Research and Supply Company.

See Chapter 10, above, for address.

The Classical Method

Canon Press
PO Box 8729
Moscow ID 83843
800-488-2034
Fax: 208-882-1568
canorder@moscow.com
www.canonpress.org

The Principle Approach

F.A.C.E.
PO Box 9588
Chesapeake VA 23321-9588
800-352-3223
Fax: 757-488-5593
info@face.net
www.face.net

Five In A Row

PO Box 707
Grandview MO 64030-0707
816-246-9252
Fax: 816-246-9253
lamberts@fiveinarow.com
www.fiveinarow.com

Far Above Rubies

All-Around Education
PO Box 11562
Montgomery AL 36111
334-278-7888
Fax: 334-273-7889
FARauthor@aol.com
http://www.farandblessed.com

Chapter 12

Business Books

From your library, or any bookstore.
Homemade Money, Barbara Brabec
Guerrilla Marketing, Jay Conrad Levinson

The Timberdoodle Company

1510 E Spencer Lk Rd
Shelton WA 98584
360-426-0672
Fax: 800-478-0672
mailbag@timberdoodle.com
www.timberdoodle.com

Creativity Press

1211 12th Street
Anacortes, WA 98221
anne@anneolwin.com
www.creativitypress.com.

F.U.N. Books

See "Preface" above.

Chapter 13

Home School High School & Beyond

Castlemoyle Books

The Hotel Revere Building

PO Box 520

Pomeroy WA 99347-0520

509-843-5009

Fax: 509-843-3183

johnr@castlemoyle.com

http://www.castlemoyle.com

Dinner's in the Freezer!

Also *Mega Cooking,* both by Jill Bond

www.amazon.com

Relationships Pure and Simple

Loring Gate Productions

610 West 28th Street

Kearney NE 68845

308-234-4689

info@loringgate.com

www.loringgate.com

Course of Study

Mantle Ministries

See address above under Chapter 7.

Other Homeschool Catalogs

Children's Books

PO Box 239
Greer SC 29652
800-344-3198
Fax: 864-968-0391
www.childrensbooks-sc.com

Christian Book Distributors

PO Box 7000
Peabody MA 01961-7000
800-247-4784
Fax: 978-977-5010
orders@christianbook.com
www.christianbook.com

Lifetime Books & Gifts

3900 Chalet Suzanne Dr
Lake Wales FL 33859-6881
863-676-6311
Fax: 863-676-2732
info@lifetimebooksandgifts.com
www.lifetimebooksandgifts.com

Endnotes

Preface

1   Bill Greer, "What is 'Unschooling'?" *F.U.N. News,* October 1994, p. 1.
2   Helen Hegener, editorial, *Home Education Magazine.*
3   Raymond and Dorothy Moore, *The Successful Homeschool Family Handbook: A Creative and Stress-Free Approach to Homeschooling* (Thomas Nelson, 1994).
4   [71.1%] Dr. Brian Ray, and the Home School Legal Defense Association, 1997.

Chapter 1
Laying Foundations
1   The method for setting and reaching goals described in this book was adapted from that of businessman Charles Givens.
2   Charlotte Mason, *An Essay towards a Philosophy of Education* (Wheaton: Tyndale House 1989).
3   William Feather, *Living Quotations for Christians* (New York: Harper & Row, 1974) p. 63.

Chapter 2
Starting Up
1   It is important that young children are not pushed into formal schooling too soon. See any of Dr. Raymond and Dorothy Moore's books, especially *Better Late than Early* or *School Can Wait.*

2   Lyric Wallwork Winik, "We are Responsible," *Parade Magazine,* March 19, 1995, p. 7.

3   *The Futurist,* January-February 1996 (World Future Society, 7910 Woodmont Ave., Suite 450, Bethesda, MD 20814, 301-656-8274, fax: 301-951-0394).

4   "Science Fiction," Zane CD Rom.

5   J. Oswald Sanders, *Living Quotations for Christians* (New York: Harper & Row, 1974).

6   William F. Russell, *Classics to Read Aloud to Your Children,* 1984.

7   Lyric Wallwork Winik, "We are Responsible," *Parade Magazine,* March 19, 1995, p. 7.

8   National Home Education Research Institute (1999).

Chapter 3
EasySchool Basics

1    $5,325, National Home Education Research Institute (1999).

2   *Strong Families, Strong Schools,* DOE, 1995.

3   Gail Riplinger, "King James for Kids," *New Age Bible Versions,* (Ararat: A.V. Publications, 1995) p. 212.

Chapter 4
Making Order

1   Personal correspondence.

Chapter 5
Planning for Success

1   Mary Kay Ash, *Mary Kay* (New York: Harper & Row, 1981) p. 79.

Chapter 6
Combining Subjects

1   James Anthony Froude, *Living Quotations for Christians,* (New York: Harper & Row, 1974) p. 108.

2   George Washington Carver, Autobiography, p. 162.

Chapter 7
Enjoying Heirlooms

1   Sherman County Times (Loup City NE, 1924).
2   Arthur Robinson Ph.D., The Robinson Self-Teaching Home School Curriculum (Oregon Institute of Science and Medicine and Althouse Press, 1997).
3   James Kilpatrick, *The Idaho Statesman*, December 21, 1989, p. 8A.

Chapter 8
Training for Eternity

1   *Norton Anthology of English Literature*, Vol. 1 (New York: Norton) p. 849.
2   Gail Riplinger, "King James for Kids," *New Age Bible Versions*, (Ararat: A.V. Publications, 1995) pp. 195-217.
3   Cyndy Shearer, *Teaching the Bible to your Children* (Greenleaf Press, 1993)

Chapter 9
Studying Science, Math, and Art

1   Claude Monet, *Modern Masters*, National Gallery of Art.
2   Ron Ranson, *Fast and Loose* video.
3   Marilyn Burns, "The 12 Most Important Things You Can Do to Be a Better Math Teacher," "Math Questions, Ask Marilyn Burns!" "Writing in Math Class, Absolutely!" *Instructor*, April 1993, April 1994, April 1995.

Chapter 10
Gleaning from History

1   Oliver Wendall Holmes, *Living Quotations for Christians*, (New York: Harper & Row, 1974) p. 63.
2   Gabriel Compayré, *The History of Pedagogy* (Boston: Heath,1885); E.L. Kemp, *History of Education* (Philadelphia: Lippincot,1901); Levi Seeley Ph.D., *History of Education* (New York: American Book Company, 1904).

Chapter 11
Mining the Methods

1   Mary Hood Ph.D., personal correspondence, July 2,1999.

2   Hood, personal correspondence, July 4, 1999.

3   Hood, F.U.N. News, 1995.

4   Dr. Raymond and Dorothy Moore, *The Successful Homeschool Family Handbook,* Thomas Nelson, 1994.

5   Ibid.

6   Caren Cornell, "Robinson," *Tips & Topics,* Summer 1998.

7   Charlotte Mason, *An Essay towards a Philosophy of Education,* (Wheaton: Tyndale House 1989).

8   Douglas Wilson, Wes Callihan, and Douglas Jones, *Classical Education & the Home School,* (Moscow: Canon Press).

9   Wilson, Callihan, and Jones.

10 Wes Callihan, "A Map for the Mind," *Practical Homeschooling,* Issue #24.

11 Ibid.

12 Horace Bushnell, *Christian Nurture,* (Cleveland: The Pilgrim Press,1994,1861, pp. 36, 119).

13 Wilson, Callihan, and Jones.

14 Ibid.

15 Lynda Coats, personal correspondence, July, 1999.

Chapter 13
Sailing through High School

1   Mary Hood Ph.D., *The Relaxed Home School,* p 87.

2   Charlotte Mason, *An Essay towards a Philosophy of Education,* (Wheaton: Tyndale House 1989).

Chapter 14
Abiding in the Vine

1   Billy Sunday, *"Billy" Sunday, The Man and His Message* (Authorized Edition, 1914) pp. 229-246.

Index

J

K

L

M

N

Narration 151, 152
National Gallery of Art 74
Nature notebooks 82, 155
Nature study
　　77, 82, 141, 143, 155
Neatness 80
New Testament 141
Notebook 65
Notebook, business 168-169
Notebook, timeline 74
Notebook ideas 163
Notebook planning 28-32
Notebooks, children 72
Nursing home ministry 87

O

O Pioneers! 77
Obedience 155
Oral math 81
Oratory education 129
Organizing 57-58, 61
Organizing, books 61
Origen 134
Outlining 99

P

Parenting, modeling 96
Paternal authority 129
Patience, parent 108
Peace 191
Peace, homeschool 155
Peer dependency 148
Pencil, drawing 118
Penmanship 43, 74
Perfect parenting patterns 126
Perfect teacher 33
Petrarch 138-139
Philosophy 135

Phonics 40-42, 53, 79, 127
Phonics based readers 42
Planning 65-72
Plato 128
Poetry 91
Politeness 136
Practical Arithmetics 90
Prayer 101-103
Praying 35, 36, 96, 191, 192
Praying the Word 193
Pre-writing 40, 44
Predigested material 152
Preparation 34
Preschool 38, 90
Primary School 141
Principle Approach 160-161
Procedures 65
Project learning 148
Pronunciation 49
Protestantism 141
Public school, transition from 146

Q

Questioning 127
Quiet time 38
Quiet time, mom 189, 191, 192
Quintillion 129, 130

R

Ratich 142
Reading 40, 41, 127, 130, 152
Reading aloud 73, 90, 112, 150
Reading aloud, high school 180
Reformation 140
Regularity and exactness 129
Relaxed homeschooling 146
Renaissance 75, 138
Repetition, of a lesson 151
Reports 91, 161
Research 54, 74, 75, 80, 91

U

V

W

Y

Z

Businesses of Interest

Classified and Display Advertising

Audio Memory

501 Cliff Drive

Newport Beach CA 92663

800-365-SING

www.audiomemory.com

Sing along and learn Grammar, World Geography, States & Capitals, Math, U.S. History, Bible, Science and more!

Joy of Learning

Customer Service: 800-490-4430

707-964-7040

learn@joyoflearning.com

www.joyoflearning.com

Discount homeschool supplies for preschool through high school including Bob Jones, Alpha Omega and *Sing Spell Read & Write*.

Professor Phonics

4700 Hubble Road

Cincinnati OH 45247

Toll Free: 866-385-0200

Fax: 513-385-7920

Sue@professorphonics.com

www.professorphonics.com

Award winning intensive phonics curriculum. Age 4 and up. Reads in 3-6 months! Begins reading in first lesson. Self-teaching interactive CD rom.

Atelier *Homeschool Art*

4615 Rancho Reposo
Del Mar CA 92014
858-481-4223
Toll free: 888-760-ARTS
Fax: 858-481-3959
arts@homeschoolart.com
www.homeschoolart.com

The *Atelier* art program was comprehensively tested to ensure outstanding results. Using video-based teaching methods, *Atelier* provides the homeschooler with unprecedented ease of use, breadth of scope, and results-oriented validation.

CENTRIFUGE LANGUAGE ARTS

3611 C.R. 100
Hesperus CO 81326
800-900-1907
eva@centricurriculum.com
www.centricurriculum.com

Complete comprehensive coverage of all six areas of language. Superior curriculum gives the best results. K-12.

Getty-Dubay Italic Handwriting Series

Portland State University
Extended Studies
Continuing Education Press
866-647-7377
8am-5pm M-F PST
press@pdx.edu
www.cep.pdx.edu

The Getty-Dubay Italic Handwriting Series for children and adults is preferred by homeschoolers, legible because it's loop-free, and effective because it makes sense. Call or email for a free brochure and desk strip.

TRISMS Homeschool Curriculum

1203 S. Delaware Place

Tulsa, OK 74104-4129

918-585-2778

Fax: 918-585-2708

Linda@trisms.com

www.trisms.com

TRISMS combines the best of unit studies with the Classical approach.
TRISMS integrated, research-based design promotes critical thinking,
abstract reasoning, written and verbal communication skills.

AIM Life Enhancers

God's Gardener

PO Box 95

Boelus NE 68820

308-996-4497

Fax: 308-996-9104

info@easyhomeschooling.net

www.easyhomeschooling.net/AIMstore.html

Build better health! Get quick energy with *AIM BarleyLife!* Cleanse
and address gastro-intestinal issues with *AIM Herbal Fiberblend!*

Homeschooling Today® magazine is the premiere educational tool and resource that more homeschooling parents are using everyday to shape the minds and lives of their own star pupils! Each bimonthly issue features dozens of practical, time-saving, ready-to-use ideas and curricula designed to give homeschooling parents real advice and practical tools that they can immediately put to use in teaching their children.

For less than the cost of a pizza dinner ($21.99 - 38% off the cover price), you will enjoy a year of practical lessons, empowering facts, and timely encouragement that will help you better raise your children. No other magazine delivers such unparalleled homeschooling support, tips, and activities as *Homeschooling Today*!

CALL TODAY for information regarding your FREE trial issue of *Homeschooling Today*!

> ...today, consider homeschooling,
> and then consider *HomeschoolingToday*!

866-804-4478
www.homeschoolingtoday.com

Why switch to BJ HomeSat/DVD?
It's easy!

Easy to teach with!

The goal of BJ HomeSat has always been to make Mom's load a little lighter. Use our menu-based Mom's Minutes to plan your lessons.

Easy to learn from!

BJ HomeSat is renowned for its powerful and stimulating content – based on proven BJU Press curriculum.

Easy to use!

The new DVD delivery offers a more convenient and portable product than our traditional satellite dish or VHS services. Just go to the on-screen menu, and in seconds you're into today's lesson.

See for yourself. Call today for our free demo DVD!

Digital Learning Network
DVD Center
2909 King Street
Jonesboro, AR 72401
www.dlnvcr.com
dvdinfo@dlnvcr.net
1.888.406.4040 (toll-free phone)
1.800.213.1700 (toll-free fax)

BJ HomeSat/DVD
distributed by...
Digital Learning NETWORK
featuring the...
VideoClassRoom service

FergNus Services is the designer of The Homeschooler's Journal and The Homeschooler's High School Journal. This award winning system has made life easier for documenting your daily homeschooling efforts since 1991.

The One Room School Box

There are Daily Subject Logs for 200 days of schooling; Field Trip Logs; a Check-off List for Yearly Requirements; Several Calendars even a year at glance Linear Schedule; Contact Lists; Note Pages; Objective/Resource Pages and Individual Library Lists and even more.

These Journals have plenty of room for logging your daily activities and subjects. The high school edition also tracks your time spent on each subject for those States that require the number of credit hours per year. There are wide NOTE Columns on each five day planning section for additional information and/or activities. To top it off they are Wire-O bound in a JELLY PROOF COVER for extra durability.

Come visit our Web Site and see other products designed and written by other homeschooling families across this country. We are a cottage industry of cottage industries. Call for additional information.

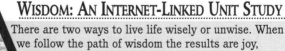

Easy Homeschooling Companion
Easy Homeschooling Techniques

God's Gardener
we plant ★ we water ★ He grows
PO Box 95 ~ Boelus NE 68820 USA
866.263.5959 ~ Fax: 308.996.9104

Specify title(s) desired. $18.95 each. Order 2 or more books for $15.00 each. FREE shipping for personal book orders. Send check, money order or credit card number with expiration date. Discounts available to booksellers, libraries and associations, Shipping charged. Bookstores, see www.faithworksonline.com.

Exceptional! Books

FROM A TIME WHEN RIGHT WAS RIGHT
AND EDUCATION MEANT EXCELLENCE

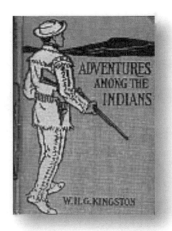

www.easyhomeschooling.net/BOOKstore.html

Enter In

To Rescue, Safety, Deliverance, Health, Prosperity

I was in a diner. The place was packed. I went outside and saw that there was a raging fire just next door! I could smell the smoke! I could feel the heat! I rushed back into the building and dialed 911, then asked the address of the building. The waitress wasn't sure. Then a man gave me an address. Nobody was excited, or in a hurry about getting out. . . . *I awoke.* . . . Are you like that crowd? There really is a fire coming nearer by the second and you will be in grave danger if you don't get out! There is an escape and His name is Jesus. Here's how to get through and out of this world alive!

- Confess your sins (failings). Tell God you want to be different. *All have sinned, and come short of the glory of God* (Rom. 3:23).
- Believe that Christ died to remove the penalty of your sins. He suffered terribly and died on a cross over two-thousand years ago for *you!* It wasn't just a movie. *God commendeth his love toward us, in that, while we were yet sinners, Christ died for us* (Rom. 5:8). *The wages of sin is death; but the gift of God is eternal life through Jesus Christ our Lord* (Rom. 6:23).
- Call on the Lord Jesus and open your heart's door and be saved from the wrath coming upon the earth. *Whosoever shall call upon the name of the Lord shall be saved* (Rom. 10:13).
- Believe and speak. *If thou shalt confess with thy mouth the Lord Jesus, and shalt believe in thine heart that God hath raised him from the dead, thou shalt be saved* (Rom. 10:9). Tell someone! Is there someone who has been praying for you? If you can't think of anyone else, tell me!
- To grow in the Lord, read your Bible often and find a church where the pure Word of God is preached. See also John 10:10, Rom. 3:10, Rom. 5:10, Rev. 3:20 and Luke 15:7.